INTRODUCTION.

Years ago some one said to me: "Madame Guyon's experience is the richest ever put upon paper."

Again and again I tried to obtain her Autobiography, or her Life by Fenelon, but failed.

I prayed: "Lord, when I am ready for Madame Guyon's Autobiography send it to me."

Years passed away, and April 9, 1898, while in the home of Pastor W. D. Fowler, of Bridgeport, Conn., he brought the two volumes to me. I had not read a dozen pages before a desire possessed me to condense the work for busy men and women. I believed the desire was of God (Psa. xxxvii. 4).

That night, ere I slept, I asked the Lord to waken me (Isa. 1. 4) with a text that would indicate His will, and my first waking thought was: "My beloved is mine, and I am His: He feedeth among the lilies" (S. of S. ii. 16). I knew He wanted me to condense the Autobiography of this "lily of the valleys" (S. of S. ii. 1) which had bloomed two hundred years ago.

Then I inquired of the Lord about a publisher, and Bro. Knapp was presented to me, though he had never published anything for me; and when I wrote him, he was delighted to do it. So the Spirit and the Word and the Providence were agreed.

Madame Guyon lived and died a Roman Catholic. She wrote the book in a prison cell, by command of her church director. Her life was a long series of persecutions; her husband's family, church dignitaries, politicians, and people combined against her and heaped upon her indignity and ignominy. All this because she loved the Lord and lived a holy life; because she served the people with intense self-sacrifice, having the gifts of healing and the discerning of spirits; because she wrote as the Spirit dictated and taught the people the art of communing with God without a prayer-book.

Yet she was more than conqueror (Rom. viii. 37) through Him who made her one of the mightiest women of the ages. The words of God to Jeremiah might also be applied to her: "Behold, I have made thee . . a defenced city, and an iron pillar, and brasen walls, against the kings of Judah, against the princes thereof, against the priests thereof, and against the people of the land. And they shall fight against thee; but they shall not prevail against thee; for I am with thee, saith the Lord, to deliver thee" (Jer. i. 18, 19).

SHE BEING DEAD YET SPEAKETH.

ABBIE C. MORROW.
JUNE 6, 1898.

MADAME GUYON.

CHAPTER I.

As you thought there were omissions of importance in the former narration of my life, I willingly comply with your desire for a more circumstantial relation. My earnest wish is to paint in true colors the goodness of God, and my own ingratitude—but it is impossible. You are unwilling I should give a minute account of my sins. But I shall leave out as few faults as possible, and depend on you to destroy it, when you have drawn those spiritual advantages which God intended for your sanctification.

This will be reached by a path that will wonderfully disappoint your expectations. On the NOTHING in man God establishes His greatest works. He destroys that He may build; for when He is about to rear His sacred temple in us, He first totally razes the vain, pompous edifice human art and power had erected, and from its horrible ruins a new structure is formed, by His power only.

Divine wisdom is unknown to many who pass in the world for persons of extraordinary illumination and knowledge. In dying to all things, and in being truly lost to them, passing forward into God, and existing only in Him, we attain true wisdom. Oh, how little are her ways known, and her dealings with her chosen servants!

Christ assures us that, except our righteousness exceed that of the Scribes and Pharisees, we shall in no case enter into the kingdom of heaven (Matt. v. 20). We see the indignation of our Lord against such. He who was the perfect pattern of tenderness and meekness, appears severe only to self-righteous people, and He publicly dishonored them. In what strange colors does He represent them, while He beholds the poor sinner with mercy, compassion and love, and declares that for them only He was come.

O Thou Source of Love! Thou dost seem so jealous of the salvation Thou hast purchased, that Thou dost prefer the sinner to the righteous! The poor sinner who beholds himself vile and wretched, and finding his state so horrible, casts himself, in his desperation, into the healing fountain, comes forth "white as wool." Whilst the self-righteous, relying on the many good works he imagines he has performed, seems to hold salvation in his own hand, and considers heaven a just reward of his merits. In the bitterness of his zeal he exclaims against all sinners, and represents the gates of mercy as barred against them. What need have such of a Saviour? Already burdened with their own merits, they bear the flattering load, whilst sinners divested of everything, fly rapidly on the wings of faith and love into their Saviour's arms, who freely bestows what He has freely promised.

You may imagine this a digression wide of the subject, but it leads insensibly to it, and shows that God accomplishes His work in persons whose self-righteousness He destroys, by totally overthrowing the proud building they had reared. The establishment of all which He proposed in coming to the world, is effected by the apparent overthrow of that very structure which He would erect; for, by means which seem to destroy

His Church, He establishes it. How strangely does He found the new dispensation! The very Legislator Himself is condemned as a malefactor, and dies an ignominious death. Oh, that we understood how opposite our self-righteousness is to the designs of God—it would be a subject for endless humiliation, and we should have an utter distrust in that which constitutes the whole of our dependence.

This being premised, it will be less difficult for you to conceive the designs of God, in the favors He has conferred on one of the most insignificant of His creatures. It pleased Him to take one most unworthy, to make known the fact that His graces are the effects of His will, not the fruits of our merits; that it is the property of His wisdom, to destroy what is proudly built, and to build what is destroyed; to make use of weak things to confound the mighty, and to employ in His service such as appear contemptible, as you will see in the narrative of the life you have enjoined me to write.

CHAPTER II.

I was born April, 1648. My parents were extremely pious, particularly my father, as many of his forefathers were saints. I was so excessively ill, after my birth, all despaired of my life, and it was some time before they could find opportunity to baptize me. I continued unhealthy until two and a half years old, when they sent me to the convent of the Ursulines for a few months.

On my return, my mother, not fond of daughters, abandoned me to the care of servants; and I should have suffered severely from their inattention, had not an all-watchful Providence been my Protector: for through my liveliness I met with various accidents. I frequently fell into a deep vault that held our fire-wood; but always escaped unhurt.

The Duchess of Montbason came to the convent of the Benedictines, when I was about four. She had a great friendship for my father, and obtained his permission that I should go to the same convent. I became her constant companion.

I was guilty of frequent irregularities in this house, and committed serious faults. Yet I had good examples, and being naturally well inclined, I quickly followed them, when there were none to turn me aside. I loved to hear God spoken of, to be at church, and to be dressed in a religious habit.

My heart glowed with fervor, and I felt a desire to suffer martyrdom. The girls of the house, to amuse themselves, and see how far this fervor would carry me, desired me to prepare for martyrdom. I found great delight in prayer, and was persuaded that this ardor, as new as pleasing, was a proof of God's love; and this inspired me with such courage I earnestly besought them to proceed, that I might enter into His sacred presence. But was there not latent hypocrisy here? Did I not imagine it possible they would not kill me, and I should have the merit of martyrdom without suffering it? It appeared so, for being placed kneeling on a cloth, and seeing a large sword lifted, which they had prepared to try me, I cried, "Hold! it is not right I should die without my father's permission." I was quickly upbraided with having said this that I might escape. I continued long disconsolate, and would receive no comfort.

At my solicitation, and on account of my falling so frequently sick, I was taken home. My mother, having a maid in whom she placed confidence, left me again to the care of servants.

Greatly is it to be lamented that mothers, inclined to piety, should commit the greatest irregularities while apparently pursuing that which should produce the most circumspect conduct.

Thus, because they experience certain sweetnesses in prayer, they would be all day at church; while their children are running to destruction at home. We glorify God most when we prevent what may offend Him. What must be the nature of that sacrifice which is the occasion of sin. God should be served in His way, not ours.

My father, who loved me tenderly, seeing how little my education was attended to, sent me to a convent of the Ursulines. I was nearly seven. In this house were two half-sisters, one by my father, the other by my mother. My father placed me under his daughter's care, a person of great capacity, exalted piety, and excellently qualified for the instruction of youth. A singular dispensation of God's love to me, and the first means of my salvation. She loved me tenderly, and had I continued in such careful hands, I should have acquired many virtuous habits.

As my father often sent for me to come home, I found at one time the Queen of England there. I was nearly eight. My father told the Queen's confessor, that if he wanted a little amusement, he might propound some questions to me. He tried me with difficult ones, to which I returned such pertinent answers, that he carried me to the Queen, and said, "Your majesty must have some diversion." She, being well pleased with my lively answers, demanded me of my father for maid of honor to the princess. But my father resisted. God caused this refusal, and turned off the stroke which might have intercepted my salvation; for weak as I was, how could I have withstood the temptations of a Court?

I went back to the Ursulines, where my good sister continued her affection. But as she was not mistress of the boarders, and I was obliged to go with them, I contracted bad habits, lying, peevishness and indevotion, passing whole days without thinking on God; though He watched continually over me. I did not remain long under the power of such vicious habits, for my sister's care recovered me.

At the end of the garden connected with this convent was a little chapel dedicated to the child Jesus. To this I betook myself for devotion; and, carrying my breakfast thither every morning, hid it behind His image; for I thought I made a considerable sacrifice in depriving myself of it. Being delicate in my choice of food, I wished to mortify myself; but found self-love still too prevalent to submit to such mortification. When they cleaned this chapel, they found behind the image what I had left there, and guessed it was I, as they had seen me go thither. God soon rewarded me with interest for this little infantine devotion.

I improved much while in health; but often I was sick, and seized with maladies as sudden as uncommon. At nine years of age, I was taken with so violent a hemorrhage, they thought I was going to die.

A little before this severe attack, my other sister became jealous, wanting to have me in her turn. Though she led a good life, she had not talent for educating children. At first she caressed me; but all her caresses made no impression upon my heart. My other sister did more with a look, than she with caresses or threatenings. As she saw that I loved her not so well as the other, she changed her fondling to rigor. She would not allow me to speak to my other sister; and when I did, had me whipped, or beat me herself. I could no longer hold out against such severe usage, and requited with apparent ingratitude all the favors of my paternal sister, going no more to see her. But this did not hinder her from giving me marks of goodness. She kindly construed my ingratitude to fear of chastisement, rather than to a bad heart.

My father took me home again. I was nearly ten. I stayed only a little while; for a nun of St. Dominie, one of my father's intimate friends, solicited him to place me in her convent, promising she would take care of me herself, having conceived a great affection for me. But she was so taken up with troublesome events, she was not at liberty to take care of me. Here I had the chicken-pox, three weeks, in which I had bad attendance, though father thought I was under excellent care. The ladies of the house had such a dread of the small-pox, as they imagined mine to be, they durst not come near me. I passed nearly all the time without seeing anybody, but a lay-sister, who only brought me my allowance of diet at set hours, and went off again. I found a Bible, and having a fondness for reading and a happy memory, I read it from morning to night, and learned the historical part. Yet, I was really unhappy in this house; for the girls distressed me with grievous persecutions. I was so neglected, as to food, that I fell away, and became emaciated.

CHAPTER III.

After eight months, my father took me home again. My mother kept me more with her; yet preferred my brother. Even when I was sick and met with anything I liked, if he demanded it, it was taken from me, and given to him, though he was in perfect health. He was continually giving me new vexations. One day he made me mount the top of the coach; threw me down on the ground, and I was much bruised. At other times he beat me. But whatever he did, however wrong, it had the most favorable construction put upon it. This soured my temper. My step-sisters by the mother, gained her good will by caressing him and persecuting me. I relapsed into lying and peevishness. With all these faults I was charitable to the poor, prayed to God assiduously, loved to hear anyone speak of Him, and to read good books.

I can not bear to hear it said, "We are not free to resist grace." I have had too long an experience. I closed up the avenues of my heart, that I might not hear that secret voice of God, calling me to Himself. I have from tenderest youth passed through a series of grievances. The girl to whose care my mother left me, in dressing my head used to beat me, and did not make me turn it but with blows. My father knew nothing of all this; his love was such he would not have suffered it. I loved him much, but feared him, so I told him nothing. My mother often teased him with complaints of me, to which he replied, "There are twelve hours in the day; she 'll grow wiser."

My father placed me in Lent among the Ursulines, to receive my first communion at Easter, in my eleventh year. And here my dear sister redoubled her care, to cause me to make the best preparation for this act of devotion. I thought now of giving myself to God in good earnest.

Easter arrived, and I received the communion with joy. I stayed till Whitsuntide. As my other sister was mistress of the second class, she demanded that in her week I should be with her. Her manners made me relax my piety. I felt no more that delightful ardor which had seized my heart at my first communion.

As I now grew tall for my age, and more to my mother's liking, she took care to deck me, to make me see company, and to take me abroad. She took an inordinate pride in that beauty with which God had formed me. Several suitors offered to me; but as I was not yet twelve, my father would not listen. I shut myself up alone every day to read.

What proved effectual to gain me over entirely to God for a time, was that a cousin passed by our house, going on a mission to Cochin, China. I happened to be taking a walk with my companions, which I seldom did. At my return he was gone. They gave me an account of his sanctity, and the things he had said. I was so touched, I was overcome with sorrow. I cried all the rest of the day and of the night.

I immediately applied myself to every part of my duty. I became so changed I would not for ever so much have had the least slip, and God did me the favor to enable me to conquer myself in many things. There were left only some remains of passion. As soon as I had given any displeasure, even to the domestics, I begged their pardon, to subdue my wrath and pride.

Wrath is the daughter of pride. A person truly humble suffers nothing to put him in a rage. Pride dies last in the soul. Passion is last destroyed in the outward conduct. A soul thoroughly dead to self, finds nothing of rage left.

There are persons who, filled with the unction of grace, and a tranquil peace, at the entrance of the resigned path of light and love, think they are come thus far. But they are greatly mistaken. There often arises in them certain motions of anger, but the sweetness of grace holds them back by a secret violence. They would easily transgress, if they gave way to these motions. There are persons who think themselves mild, because nothing thwarts them. Of such I am not speaking: for the mildness which has never been proved is often only counterfeit. Those persons who, when unmolested, appear saints, are no sooner exercised by vexing occurrences, than there starts up in them strange faults, which they had thought dead; and which only lay dormant because nothing awakened them.

I followed my religious exercises. I shut myself up all day to read and pray. I read the works of Francis de Sales and the life of Madame de Chantal. There I first learned what mental prayer was. I prayed earnestly to God to give me the gift of prayer. All that I saw in the life of M. de Chantal charmed me; and I thought I ought to do everything I saw in it. One day reading that she had put the name of Jesus on her heart, to follow the counsel, "Set me as a seal upon thy heart," and had taken a red-hot iron, whereupon the holy name was engraven, I was afflicted that I could not do the same. I wrote that sacred name, in large characters, on a piece of paper, then with ribbands and a needle I fastened it to my skin; and it continued a long time.

CHAPTER IV.

No sooner was my father returned home, than he fell into a violent illness. My mother was also indisposed. I was all alone with him, ready to render him every kind of service. I performed the most menial offices unperceived by him, when the servants were not at hand; as well to mortify myself as to pay due honor to what Christ said, that He came not to be ministered to, but to minister. When he made me read to him, I read with such heartfelt devotion he was surprised.

My cousin, a niece of my father, who lived with us, helped to support me in good sentiments. Her fortune being equal neither to her birth nor her virtue, she did with affection what her condition obliged her to. My mother grew jealous, fearing I should love her too well. My cousin fell ill; mother took that occasion to send her home, a stroke to my heart, and that grace which began to dawn in me.

Though my mother acted thus, she was a virtuous woman. God permitted it for my exercise. She was most charitable. She not only gave away the surplus, but even the necessaries of the house. Never were the needy neglected. She sometimes gave the last penny, though she had so large a family to maintain, yet did not fail in her faith.

My mother's only care about me had been to have me in the house, one material point for a girl. And this habit of being so constantly within, proved of great service after my marriage.

After my cousin left I continued some time in sentiments of piety. God granted me the grace to forgive those who out of envy, traduced me; and I spoke well of them as occasion offered. I was enabled to suffer with resignation and patience, so long as I continued the practice of mental prayer.

Nearly a year after, we went to the country. My father took with us one of his relations, an accomplished young gentleman. He had a great desire to marry me; but father, who had resolved not to give me to any near kinsman, put him off. As this young gentleman was devout, and every day said the office of the Virgin, I said it with him; and to have time for it, left off prayer, which was the first inlet of evil.

I became cold toward God. All my old faults revived, to which I added excessive vanity. The love I began to have for myself, extinguished in me the love of God. Oh, my God, if the value of prayer were but known, the great advantage to the soul from conversing with Thee, everyone would be assiduous in it. It is a strong hold into which the enemy can not enter. He may attack it, besiege it, make a noise about its walls; but while we are faithful, he can not hurt us.

Let the poor come, let the ignorant and carnal come, let the children without reason or knowledge come, let the dull or hard hearts which can retain nothing come to the practice of prayer, and they shall become wise. Come to this Fountain of all good, without complaining to weak and impotent creatures, who cannot help you; come to prayer; lay before God your troubles, beg His grace—and above all, that you may love Him.

I forsook the Fountain of living water when I left off prayer. I became as a vineyard exposed to pillage, whose hedges torn down give liberty to all to ravage it. I began to seek in the creature what I had found in God.

He left me to myself, because I first left Him; and it was His will by permitting me to sink into the horrible pit, to make me feel the necessity of approaching Him in prayer. I fell into the greatest of all misfortunes; for I wandered yet further and further from God.

I became more passionate than I had ever been, as age gave force to nature. I was frequently guilty of lying. Vanity now resumed its seat in my heart. I passed much of my time before a looking-glass. I found much pleasure in viewing myself therein. Instead of making use of this exterior God had given me, that I might love Him the more, it became the means of a vain complacency. All seemed beautiful in my person. I saw not that it covered a polluted soul. This rendered me so inwardly vain, I doubt whether any ever exceeded me therein; but there was an affected modesty in my outward deportment that would have deceived the world.

My high esteem for myself made me find faults in everyone else of my own sex. I had no eyes but to see my own good qualities, and discover the defects of others. I hid my own faults, or if I remarked any, I excused, and even figured them as perfections. Every idea I had of others and of myself was false. I loved reading to such excess, particularly romances, that I spent whole days and nights at them; sometimes the day broke whilst I continued to read, so that I almost lost the habit of sleeping. I was ever eager to get to the end of the book, in hopes of finding something to satisfy a craving I found within; but my thirst for reading only increased the more I read. These books are strange inventions to destroy youth; for if they caused no other hurt than the loss of precious time, is not that too much?

Meanwhile, through Thy abundant mercy, O my God, Thou didst knock at the door of my heart. I was often penetrated with lively sorrow and shed abundance of tears. I was afflicted to find my state so different from what it was when I enjoyed Thy sacred presence; but my tears were fruitless and my grief vain. I could not of myself get out of this wretched state. When I tried I only sunk the deeper, and each attempt only made me see my own impotence, and rendered me more afflicted.

Oh, how much compassion has this sad experience given me for sinners, as it taught me why so few of them emerge from the miserable state into which they have fallen. The devil is outrageous against prayer, and those that exercise it; because he knows it is the means of taking his prey from him. He lets us undergo all the austerities we will. But no sooner does one enter into a spiritual life, a life of prayer, but he must prepare for strange crosses; as all manner of persecutions and contempts in this world are reserved for that life.

I loved to hear anyone speak of God, and would never tire of the conversation. When my father spoke of Him, I was transported with joy; and when he and my mother went on any pilgrimage, and were to set off early in the morning, I either did not go to bed or hired the girls to wake me early. My father's conversation at such times was of divine matters, which afforded me the highest delight. I loved the poor, and was charitable, even whilst so faulty. How strange may this seem to some, and how hard to reconcile things so opposite.

CHAPTER V.

Afterwards we came to Paris, where my vanity increased. No course was spared to make me appear to advantage. One who had asked for me in marriage for several years, my father, for family reasons, had refused. But, a fear lest I should leave my country, together with the affluent circumstances of this gentleman, induced my father, in spite of his own and my mother's reluctance, to promise me to him, which was done without consulting me. They made me sign the marriage articles without knowing what they were; though I was well pleased with the thoughts of marriage, flattering myself with a hope of being set at liberty, and delivered from the ill-treatment of my mother.

I did not see my spouse-elect, at Paris, till three days before our marriage. I caused masses to be said all the time after my being contracted, to know the will of God. Oh, my God, how great was Thy goodness, to bear with me, and allow me to pray to Thee with as much boldness, as if I had been one of Thy friends.

The joy of our nuptials was universal through our village. Amidst this general rejoicing, there appeared none sad but myself. I could neither laugh nor eat, so much was I depressed, though I knew not the cause. But it was a foretaste God gave me of what was to befall me. The remembrance of my desire to be a nun, came pouring in upon me. All who came to compliment me could not forbear rallying me, because I wept bitterly. I answered: "Alas! I had desired to be a nun; why then am I married? And by what fatality has such a revolution befallen me?" No sooner was I at the house of my spouse than I perceived it would be a house of mourning. The manner of living was different from that in my father's house. My mother-in-law, a widow, regarded nothing else but economy; whereas, at my father's house they lived in great elegance; and what my husband and mother-in-law called pride, I called politeness.

At the time of my marriage I was a little past fifteen. My surprise increased when I saw I must lose what I had acquired with so much application. At my father's house we were obliged to behave in a genteel way, and speak with propriety. Here they never hearkened to me, but to contradict and find fault. If I spoke well, they said it was to give them a lesson. If I spoke my sentiments, they said it was to enter into a dispute. They put me to silence in a shameful manner, and scolded me from morning until night. My mother-in-law conceived such a desire to oppose me in everything, that, in order to vex me, she made me perform the most humiliating offices. All her occupation was to thwart me, and she inspired the like sentiment in her son. They would make persons far my inferiors take places above me. My mother, who had a high sense of honor, could not endure that. And when she heard it from others, for I told her nothing, she chided me, thinking I did not know how to keep my rank, and that I had no spirit. I durst not tell her how it was; but I was almost ready to die with the agonies of grief and vexation. And what aggravated them all, was the remembrance of the persons who had proposed for me, the difference, the love they had for me, their agreeableness and politeness. All this made my position doleful, my burden intolerable. My mother-in-law upbraided me in regard to my family, and spoke incessantly to the disadvantage of my father and mother. I never went to see them, but I had bitter speeches to bear on my return.

My mother complained that I did not come often to see her, did not love her, was alienated from my own family, and too much attached to my husband. I had heavy suffering to undergo on both sides.

My husband obliged me to stay all day in my mother-in-law's room, without any liberty of retiring into my own, so I had not a moment's respite to breathe. She spoke disadvantageously of me to everybody, to lessen the affection some entertained for me, and galled me with the grossest affronts before the finest company. This had not the effect she wanted; for the more patiently they saw me bear it, the higher esteem they had for me.

To complete my affliction, they presented me with a waiting-maid who was everything with them. She kept me in sight like a governess, and treated me in a strange manner. For the most part, I bore with patience these evils. But sometimes I let some hasty answers escape me, which was a source of grievous crosses to me, and violent reproaches for a long time. When I went out, the footmen had orders to give an account of everything I did. I began to eat the bread of sorrows, and mingle tears with my drink. At the table they always did something to me, which covered me with confusion. I could not forbear tears, and had a double confusion,— one for what they said, and the other for not being able to refrain weeping. I had no one to confide in who might share my affliction, and assist me to bear it. When I would impart some hint of it to my mother, I drew upon myself new crosses, so that I resolved to have no confidant of my trouble. It was not from any natural cruelty that my husband treated me thus; for he loved me passionately, but he was hasty, and my mother-in-law continually irritated him about me.

Such weighty crosses made me return to God. I began to deplore the sins of my youth; for since my marriage I had not committed any voluntarily. I laid aside the reading of romances. Novels appeared to me only full of deceit. I put away even indifferent books. I resumed the practice of prayer, and endeavored to offend God no more. I felt His love gradually recovering the ascendant in my heart, and banishing every other. Yet I had still an intolerable vanity and self-complacency, my most grievous and obstinate sin.

My crosses doubled every day. My mother-in-law, not content with the bitterest speeches in public and private, would break out in a passion about the smallest trifles, and scarcely be pacified for a fortnight together. These so impaired the vivacity of my nature, that I became like a lamb that is shorn. As my age differed from theirs (my husband was twenty-two years older than I), I saw that there was no probability of changing their humors, fortified with years. As I found that whatever I said was offensive, I knew not what to do. One day, weighed down by grief and in despair, being alone, I was tempted to cut out my tongue, that I might no longer irritate those who seized every word I uttered with rage and resentment. But Thou, O God, didst stop me and showed me my folly.

My condition in marriage was rather that of a slave than of a free person. My husband was gouty. This malady caused me many crosses. He had the gout twice the first year, six weeks each time. He was so plagued with it, that he came not out of his room, nor often out of his bed. I carefully attended him, though so young. He had that foible, that when anyone said anything to him against me, he flew into a passion. It was the conduct of providence over me; for he was a man of reason and loved me much. When I was sick, he was inconsolable. Had it not been for my mother-in-law, and the girl I have spoken of, I should have been happy with him. For most men have their passions, and it is the duty of a woman to bear them peaceably, without irritating them by cross replies.

The first year I did not make proper use of my afflictions. I was still vain. I sometimes lied, to excuse myself to my husband and mother-in-law. Sometimes I fell into a passion. But Thou, O my God, opened my eyes. I found in Thee reasons for suffering, which I never found in the creature. I afterwards saw clearly and with joy that this conduct, unreasonable and mortifying, was necessary; for had I been applauded here as at my father's, I should have grown intolerably proud. I had a fault common to our sex, I could not hear a beautiful woman praised without finding fault in her.

Just before the birth of my first child, they were induced to take great care of me, and my crosses were mitigated. Indeed, I was so ill, it was enough to excite the compassion of the most indifferent. They had so great a desire of having children to inherit their fortune they were continually afraid lest I should hurt myself. I took a fever, which rendered me so weak that I could scarcely bear to be moved, to have my bed made. When I began to recover, an imposthume on my breast, laid open in two places, gave me great pain. Yet all these maladies seemed only a shadow of troubles, in comparison with those I suffered in the family; which daily increased. I was also subject to violent headaches. Life was so wearisome that those maladies which were thought mortal did not frighten me.

The sickness improved my appearance, and served to increase my vanity. I was glad to call forth expressions of regard; and when in the street, I pulled off my mask out of vanity, and drew off my gloves to show my hands. Could there be greater folly? After falling into these weaknesses, I used to weep bitterly at home; yet when occasion offered, I fell into them again.

My husband lost considerably. This cost me strange crosses; not that I cared for the losses, but I seemed to be the butt of all the ill-humors of the family. It would require a volume to describe all I suffered.

I would be totally silent with regard to their treatment of me, were it not for the injunction you have laid upon me, as my spiritual director, to relate everything.

I now dressed my hair in modest manner, never painted, and to subdue the vanity which still had possession of me, I rarely looked in the glass. My reading was confined to books of devotion, such as Thomas a' Kempis and Francis de Sales. I read these aloud to the servants, whilst the maid was dressing my hair; and suffered myself to be dressed as she pleased, which took away the occasions wherein my vanity used to be exercised. I knew not how things were; but they always thought all well in point of dress. How often have I gone to church, not so much to worship God as to be seen. Other women, jealous of me, affirmed that I painted; and told my confessor, who chided me for it, though I assured him I was innocent. I spoke in my own praise, and sought to raise myself by depreciating others. Yet these faults gradually decreased; for I was sorry afterwards for having committed them. I often examined myself strictly, writing down my faults from week to week, to see how I improved. But, alas! this labor, though fatiguing, was of little service, because I trusted in my own efforts. I wished indeed to be reformed, but my good desires were languid.

At one time my husband's absence was so long, my crosses and vexations at home so great, that I determined to go to him. My mother-in-law strongly opposed it; but this once my father interfering, she let me go. I found he had liked to have died. Through vexation and fretting, he was much changed; for he could not finish his affairs, having no liberty in attending to them, keeping himself concealed at the Hotel de Longueville, where Madame de Longueville was extremely kind to me. As I came publicly, he was in great fear lest I should make him known. In a rage he bade me return; but love, and my long absence from him, surmounting every other reason, he relented, and suffered me to stay. He kept me eight days, without letting me stir out of his chamber; till, fearing the effects of such a close confinement, he desired me to walk in the garden.

I can not express all the kindness I met with in this house. All the domestics served me with emulation, and applauded me. Everyone studied how to divert or oblige me. Outwardly everything appeared agreeable, but chagrin so ruffled my husband, that I had continually something to bear. Sometimes he threatened to throw the supper out of the window; but I said he would then do me an injury, as I had a keen appetite. I made him laugh, and laughed with him. This appeased and diverted him. Before that, melancholy prevailed over all my endeavors and over the love he had for me. But God armed me with patience, and gave me grace to return him no answer; so that the devil was forced to retire in confusion, through the signal assistance of that grace.

I fell into a languishing state; I loved God and was

unwilling to displease Him, and was inwardly grieved on account of that vanity I found myself unable to eradicate. These inward distresses, together with oppressive crosses, threw me into sickness; and as I was unwilling to incommode the Hotel de Longueville, I had myself moved to another house. The disease proved violent and tedious, so the physicians despaired of my life. The priest, a pious man, seemed fully satisfied with the state of my mind, and said I should die a saint. At midnight they ministered the sacrament to me, hourly expecting my departure. It was a scene of general distress. There were none indifferent to my death but myself. I beheld it without fear. My husband was inconsolable, and in an agony of grief, when he saw there was no hope. I recovered almost miraculously; and this disorder proved a great blessing; for beside great patience under violent pains, it served to instruct me in the emptiness of worldly things; detached me from myself, and gave me new courage to suffer. The love of God gathered strength in my heart, with a desire to please and be faithful to Him. I had yet six months to drag along with a slow fever. It was thought it would terminate in death.

CHAPTER VI.

After long languishing I regained my health; about which time my dear mother departed this life in good tranquility.

I now applied myself to my duties, never failing to practice prayer twice a day. I watched, to subdue my spirit continually. I went to visit the poor, assisting them in their distempers and distresses.

A lady, an exile, came to my father's house and stayed a long time. She was one of true piety and inward devotion. She had a great esteem for me, because I desired to love God, and employed myself in exterior works of charity. She remarked that I had the virtues of an active and bustling life; but had not attained the simplicity of prayer she experienced. I did not understand her. He example instructed me more than her words. I observed in her a great enjoyment of the presence of God. This I tried, by studied reflection, to attain, but to little purpose. I wanted by my own efforts what I could not acquire but in ceasing from all efforts.

My father's nephew returned from Cochin, China. I was exceedingly glad to see him, remembering what good his first passing by had done me. The lady above mentioned too rejoiced; they understood each other immediately, and conversed in spiritual language. This excellent relation charmed me. I admired his continual prayer, without being able to comprehend it. I endeavored to think on God without intermission, to utter prayers and ejaculations, but could not acquire, by all my toil, what God at length gave me Himself, and which is experienced only in simplicity. My cousin did all he could to attach me more strongly to God. The purity he observed in me from the corruptions of the age, the abhorrence of sin at a time of life when others begin to relish the pleasures of it (I was not eighteen), gave him great tenderness for me. I complained to him of my faults ingenuously; but as the difficulties I found, of entirely reforming, abated my courage, he exhorted me to persevere. He would have introduced me into a more simple manner of prayer, but I was not prepared for it.

His prayers were more effectual than his words; for no sooner was he gone, than Thou, O my Divine Love, manifested Thy favor. The desire I had to please Thee, the tears I shed, the pains I underwent, the labors I sustained, and the little fruit I reaped from them, moved Thee with compassion. Thy goodness granted me in a moment, what all my own efforts could never procure. Beholding me rowing with such laborious toil, the breath of Thy divine operations turned in my favor, and carried me full sail over this sea of affliction.

God permitted a religious person, of St. Francis, to pass by my father's habitation. He had intended going another way, shorter and more commodious; but a secret power changed his design. The conquest of my soul was God's design. As soon as he arrived in our country, he came to see my father, who was rejoiced. I was about to be delivered of my second son, and my father was dangerously ill. They concealed his sickness from me, on account of my condition; till an indiscreet person told me. I arose, weak as I was, and went to see him at the hazard of my life; and a dangerous illness it cost me. My father was recovered enough to give me new marks of his affection. I told him of the strong desire I had to love God. As he had a great fondness for me, he thought he could not give me a more solid indication thereof, than in procuring me an acquaintance with this worthy man, and urged me to go and see him.

I took a kinswoman with me, and went. He seemed confused; for he was reserved towards women. Being newly come out of a five years' solitude, he was surprised that I was the first to address him. He spoke not a word for some time. I did not hesitate to tell him my difficulties about prayer. He replied: "It is because you seek without what you have within. Seek God in your heart, and you will there find Him."

Having said these words, he left. They were like a dart. Through my heart I felt a deep wound, so delightful that I desired not to be cured. These words discovered to me what was in my heart, which I had not enjoyed for want of knowing it. O my Lord, Thou wast in my heart, and demanded only a turning of my mind inward, to make me perceive Thy presence. Oh, Infinite Goodness! how was I running hither and thither to seek Thee, my life a burden to me, though my happiness was within myself. I was poor in the midst of riches, and ready to perish with hunger, near a table plentifully spread. This I now experienced, for Thou becamest my King, and my heart Thy kingdom, wherein Thou didst reign supreme, and performed all Thy sacred will.

I told this good man I did not know what he had done to me. My heart was quite changed. God was there; for from that moment He had given me an experience of His presence in my soul; not by thought or application of mind, but as a thing really possessed after the sweetest manner. I experienced these words in the Canticles: "Thy name is as precious ointment poured forth; therefore do the virgins love Thee" (S. of S. i. 3). I felt in my soul an unction which healed in a moment all my wounds. I slept not that whole night, because Thy love, O my God, flowed in me like delicious oil, and burned as a fire to devour all that was left of self. I was suddenly so altered I was hardly known either by myself or others. I found no longer those troublesome faults or reluctances. They all disappeared, being consumed like chaff in a great fire.

I now became desirous that the instrument hereof might be my director. This good father upon my earnest request said he would pray to God, and desired that I should do so, too. As he was at prayer, it was said to him, "Fear not that charge; she is my spouse." This affected me greatly. After this he consented to my request.

Nothing now was more easy to me than prayer. Hours passed like moments, while I could hardly do anything but pray. The fervency of my love allowed no intermission. It was a prayer of rejoicing and possessing, devoid of busy imaginations and forced reflections; a prayer of the will, and not of the head, wherein the taste of God was so great, so pure, unblended and uninterrupted, that it absorbed the power of my soul into a profound recollection without act or discourse. For I had now no sight but of Christ alone.

This sovereign power, the will, absorbed memory and understanding, and concentrated them in LOVE;—not but they still subsisted, but their operations were imperceptible and passive. So the rising of the sun does not extinguish the stars, but absorbs them in the lustre of his imcomparable glory.

Such was the prayer given me at once, far above ecstacies, transports or visions, which are less pure, and more subject to illusion or deceits from the enemy.

Visions are in the inferior powers, therefore the soul must not rely upon them, or be retarded by them. They are but favors and gifts,—the Giver alone must be our object and aim.

"Satan transforms himself into an angel of light" (II. Cor. xi. 18) with such as are fond of visions, and lay stress on them; because they are apt to convey a vanity to the soul, or hinder it from humbly attending to God only.

Ecstacies may be a kind of spiritual sensuality, wherein the soul letting itself go too far, by reason of the sweetness in them, falls imperceptibly into decay. The crafty enemy presents such interior elevations and raptures, for baits to entrap the soul; to render it sensual, to fill it with vanity and self-love, to fix its esteem and attention on the gifts of God, and to hinder it from following Jesus Christ in the way of renunciation and death to all things.

Oh, Thou Word made flesh, whose silence is inexpressible eloquence, Thou canst never be misapprehended or mistaken. Thou becomest the life of our life, and the soul of our soul. How infinitely is Thy language above all the utterances of human articulation. Thy adorable power, all efficacious in the soul, communicates itself through us to others, and as a divine seed becomes fruitful to eternal life.

CHAPTER VII

I wrote an account of my wonderful change to that good father who had been the instrument of it. It filled him with joy and astonishment. What penances did the love of suffering induce me to undergo! I was impelled to deprive myself of the most innocent indulgences; all that could gratify my taste was denied it, and I took everything that could mortify and disgust it, so that my appetite, which had been extremely delicate, was conquered. I could scarcely prefer one thing to another.

I dressed loathsome sores and wounds, at first with the greatest difficulty, but as my aversion ceased, and I could stand the most offensive things, other employment opened to me. For I did nothing of myself, but was wholly governed by my Sovereign.

When that good father asked me how I loved God, I answered: "Far more than the most passionate lover his beloved." This love of God occupied my heart so constantly and so strongly I could think of nothing else. I judged nothing else worthy of my thoughts.

The good father was an excellent preacher. He preached in the parish to which I belonged. I was so absorbed in God, I could neither open my eyes nor hear anything he said. I found that Thy Word, O my God, made its own impress on my heart, and had its effect, without the mediation of words. I have found it so ever since, but after a different manner, according to the states I have passed through. So deeply was I settled in the inward spirit of prayer, that I could scarce any more pronounce the vocal prayers.

I now quitted all company, bade farewell forever to all plays and diversions, dancing, unprofitable walks and parties of pleasure. For two years I had left off dressing my hair; it became me, and my husband approved it. My only pleasure now was to steal some moments to be alone with my only Love! All other pleasure was a pain. I lost not Thy presence, which was given me by a continual infusion, not by the efforts of the head, or by force in meditating on God, but in the will, where I tasted with unutterable sweetness the enjoyment of the beloved object; yet not as I came to do afterward, by an essential union, but by a union in the will, which brought me to discern, in a happy experience, that the soul was created to enjoy its God.

The union of the will subjects the soul to God, conforms it to all His pleasure, causes self-will gradually to die, and drawing with it the other powers, by means of the love with which it is filled, causes them gradually to be reunited in the Center, and lost therein, as to their own nature and operations.

This loss is called the annihilation of the powers, for though they still subsist, they seem annihilated to us; in proportion as love fills and inflames, it surmounts all the activities of the will, subjecting it to God, in such sort that when the soul is docile, and leaves itself to be purified, and emptied of all it has opposite to the will of God, it finds itself, by little and little, detached from every emotion of its own, and placed in a holy indifference, wishing nothing but what God wills. This never can be effected by the activity of our own will, though employed in continual acts of resignation; because these, though virtuous, are so far one's own actions, and cause the will to subsist in a kind of separate distinction from God.

When the will of the creature entirely submits to that of the Creator, suffering freely and voluntarily, and yielding only to the Divine will, suffering itself to be totally destroyed by the operations of love; this absorbs the will into itself, consummates it in that of God, and purifies it from all narrowness, dissimilitude, and selfishness.

The case is the same with the other two powers, faith and hope. Faith so strongly seizes on the understanding, as to make it decline all reasonings, all illuminations and illustrations, which sufficiently demonstrates how far visions, revelations, ecstacies, etc., differ from this, and hinder the soul from being lost in God. For though by them it appears lost in Him for some transient moments, yet it is not a true loss, since the soul which is entirely lost in God finds itself again no more.

The memory finds all its little activities surmounted by degrees, and absorbed in hope, and finally the powers are all concentrated and lost in pure love, which engulfs them into itself by means of their sovereign, the WILL; for the will is the sovereign of the powers, as love is the queen of the virtues, and unites them all in herself.

This reunion is called the central union, because that by means of the will and love, all are reunited in the center of the soul in God, our ultimate end. "He who dwelleth in love, dwelleth in God, for God is love" (I. Jno. iv. 16).

This union of my will to Thine, O my God, and this ineffable presence was so sweet and powerful, I was compelled to yield to its delightful power, strict and severe to my minutest faults.

My senses were continually mortified, and under perpetual restraint. To conquer the senses totally, deny them the smallest relaxation, until victory is complete.

Those who content themselves in practicing great outward austerities, and yet indulge their senses in what is called innocent and necessary, remain forever unsubdued. Austerities, however severe, will not conquer the senses. To destroy their power, the most effectual means is to deny them firmly what will please, and persevere in this, until they are without desire or repugnance. But if we grant them any relaxation, we act like one who, under pretext of strengthening a man, condemned to be starved to death, should give him from time to time a little nourishment, which would prolong his torments, and postpone his death.

It is the same with the death of the senses, the powers, the understanding, and self-will; for if we do not eradicate every remains of self in these, we support them in a dying life to the end. This state and its termination are clearly set forth by Paul. He speaks of bearing about in the body the dying of the Lord Jesus (II. Cor. iv. 10). But, lest we should rest here, he fully distinguishes this from the state of being dead, and having our life hid with Christ in God.

He who is thus dead has no further need of mortification; for the end of mortification is accomplished in him, and all is become new. It is an unhappy error in those who have arrived at a conquest of the bodily senses, through unremitted mortification, that they should still continue attached to the exercise; they should rather drop their attention thereto, and remain indifferent, accepting with equality the good or the bad, the sweet or the bitter, and bend their whole attention to a labor of greater importance—the mortification of the mind and self-will, beginning by dropping all activity of self, which can never be done without the most profound prayer; no more than the death of the senses can be perfected without profound recollection joined to mortification. Recollection is the chief means whereby we attain a conquest of the senses, as it separates us from them, and sweetly saps the cause from whence they derive their influence.

The more Thou didst augment my love, and my patience, O my Lord, the less respite had I from the most oppressive crosses; but love rendered them easy to bear. O ye poor souls, who exhaust yourselves with needless vexation, seek God in your hearts, and find a speedy end to all your troubles; for the increase of crosses will increase your delight.

Love, at the beginning, athirst for mortification impelled me to seek and invent various kinds, and as soon as the bitterness of any new mode of mortification was exhausted, another kind was pointed to me, and I was led to pursue it. Divine love so enlightened my heart, and so scrutinized its secret springs, that the smallest defects became exposed. If I was about to speak, something wrong was pointed to me; if I kept silence, faults were discovered—in every action, in mortifications, penances, alms-giving, retirement, I was faulty. When I walked, I observed something wrong; if I spoke in my own favor, I saw pride. If I said within myself, "Alas, I will speak no more," here was self. Pure love always found matter for reproof in me, and was jealous that nothing should escape unnoticed. Not that I was particularly attentive over myself. I waited continually upon God, and He watched incessantly over me, and so ·ed me by His providence, that I forgot all things. I could scarcely go about self-examination; when I attempted it all ideas of myself immediately disappeared, and I found myself occupied with my ONE OBJECT, without distinction of ideas. I was absorbed in peace inexpressible; I saw by faith that God wholly possessed me; but I did not reason about it.

It must not be supposed that Divine Love suffered my faults to go unpunished. O Lord! with what rigor dost Thou punish the most faithful, the most loving and beloved of Thy children. Not externally, for this would be inadequate to the smallest fault, in a soul that God is about to purify radically; and the punishments it can inflict on itself are rather gratifications than otherwise. The manner in which He corrects His chosen, must be felt, or it is impossible to conceive how dreadful it is. It is an internal burning, a secret fire, sent from God to purge away the fault, giving extreme pain, until this purification is effected. It is like a dislocated joint, in incessant torment, until the bone is replaced. This pain is so severe, that the soul would do anything to satisfy God for the fault, and rather be torn in pieces than endure the torment. Sometimes she flies to others for consolation, but thereby she frustrates God's designs. It is of the utmost consequence to know what use to make of the distress, as the whole of one's spiritual advancement depends thereon. We should at these seasons of internal anguish, obscurity and mourning, co-operate with God, and endure this consuming torture in its utmost extent, without attempting to lessen or increase it; but bear it passively, nor seek to satisfy God by anything we can do of ourselves. To continue passive at such a time is extremely difficult, and requires great firmness and courage. I knew some who never advanced further because they grew impatient, and sought means of consolation.

CHAPTER VIII.

The treatment of my husband and mother-in-law, however rigorous and insulting, I now bore silently. This was not so difficult, for the greatness of my interior occupation rendered me insensible to all the rest; yet there were times when I was left to myself. And then I could not refrain from tears, when they fell violently on me. I did the lowest offices for them, to humble myself. Yet all this did not win their favor. When they were in a rage, although I could not find that I had given them any occasion for it, yet I did not fail to beg their pardon, and even that of the girl I have spoken of. Her arrogance rose to that height, that I would not have treated the meanest slave as she treated me.

One day, as she was dressing me, she pulled me roughly, and spoke insolently. I said: "It is not on my account that I answer you, for you give me no pain, but lest you should act thus before persons to whom it would give offence. Moreover, as I am your mistress, God is assuredly offended therewith" She left me, and ran like a mad woman to my husband, telling him she would stay no longer, I treated her so ill, and that I hated her for the care she took of him. I saw my husband coming like a lion, for he was in a rage. I thought he was going to strike me; I awaited the blow with tranquility; he threatened me with his uplifted crutch; I thought he was going to knock me down; and holding myself closely to God, I beheld it without pain. He did not strike me, for he had presence of mind enough to see what an indignity it would be; but in his rage he threw it at me. It fell near me, but did not touch me; after which he discharged himself in such language, as if I had been the most infamous of creatures. I kept a profound silence, being recollected in the Lord, to suffer for His love all these things.

The girl came in. At sight of her his rage redoubled. I kept near to God, disposed to suffer what He would permit. My husband ordered me to beg her pardon, which I readily did, and appeased him. I went presently into my dear closet, where I no sooner was, than my Divine Director impelled me to make this girl a present, which I did. She was astonished, but her heart was too hard to be gained. She cried me down, and made complaints of me to everybody. But all this redounded to my honor and her disgrace. Sometimes she ran into the street, crying out: "Am not I unhappy to have such a mistress?" People gathered about her to know what I had done, and she answered, I had not spoken to her all the day. They laughed, and said: 'She has done you no great harm, then."

My husband was out of humor with my devotion. "What," said he, "you love God so much that you love me no longer." I endeavored to please him in everything he could require of me. God gave me such a purity of soul that I had not a bad thought. Sometimes my husband said to me: "One sees plainly that you never lose the presence of God."

The world, seeing I quitted it, persecuted and ridiculed me. I was its entertainment, and the subject of its fables. It could not bear that a woman, scarce twenty, should thus make war against it, and overcome. My mother-in-law took part with the world, and blamed me for not doing things, that in her heart she would have been highly offended had I done them. I was as one lost, and alone; so little communion had I with the creature. I seemed to experience literally the words, "I live, yet not I, but Christ liveth in me" (Gal. ii. 20); for He was the soul of my soul, and the life of my life. His operations were so powerful, sweet, and secret, I could not express them. We went into the country, on business. Oh! what unutterable communications did I there experience in retirement!

I was insatiable for prayer; I arose at four to pray. I went far to the church, so situated that the coach could not come to it. There was a steep hill to go down and another to ascend. All that cost me nothing; I had such a longing desire to meet God, who on His part was graciously forward to give Himself to His poor creature, and to do even visible miracles. Such as saw me lead a life so different from the women of the world, said I was a fool. They attributed it to stupidity. Sometimes they said: "What can all this mean? Some people think this lady has parts, but nothing of them appears." For if I went into company, often I could not speak; so much was I engaged with the Lord, as not to attend to anything else.

The good father I have spoken of, who was the instrument of my conversion, made me acquainted with Genevieve Granger, prioress of the Benedictines, one of the great servants of God. She proved of great service to me.

My husband, mother-in-law, and confessor, now ordered me to leave off prayer, and the exercise of piety; but I could not. Even when I was in company, the Lord seized my heart powerfully. There was a conversation within me, very different from that without. I did what I could to hinder it from appearing, but the presence of so great a Master manifested itself, even on my countenance. And that pained my husband. I did what I could to hinder it from being noticed, but was not able to hide it. I was so inwardly occupied I knew not what I ate.

I had often grievous fits of sickness and no consolation in life, but in the practice of prayer, and in seeing Mother Granger. My confessor stirred up my husband and mother-in-law to hinder me from praying. They watched me from morning till night. I durst not go from my mother-in-law's chamber or my husband's bedside. When my husband and mother-in-law played at cards, if I did but turn to the fire, they watched to see if I continued my work or shut my eyes. If I closed them, they would be in a fury against me for hours. When my husband went abroad, he would not allow me to pray in his absence. Sometimes, after he was just gone out, returning immediately, if he found me in my closet, he would be in a rage.

There is hardly a torment equal to that of being ardently drawn to retirement, and not having it in one's power to be retired. But, O my God, the war they raised, to hinder me from loving Thee, did but augment my love; and while they were striving to prevent my addresses to Thee, Thou drewest me into an inexpressible silence; and the more they labored to separate me from Thee, the more closely didst Thou unite me to Thyself. The flame of Thy love was kindled, and kept up by everything that was done to extinguish it.

Often through compliance I played at piquet with my husband, and was even more interiorly attracted than if I had been at church. I was scarce able to contain the fire which burned in my soul, which had all the fervor of what men call love, but nothing of its impetuosity; for the more ardent, the more peaceable it was. This fire gained strength from everything that was done to suppress it. And the spirit of prayer was increased, from their contrivances to disallow me any time for practicing it. I loved, without considering a motive for loving; for nothing passed in my head, but much in the innermost recesses of my soul. I thought not about any recompense, gift, or favor. The Well-Beloved was Himself the only object which attracted my heart. I could not contemplate His attributes. I knew nothing else, but to love and to suffer. Oh, ignorance more truly learned than any science of the doctors, since it taught me so well Christ crucified, and brought me in love with His holy cross. As all this passed in the will, the imagination and the understanding being absorbed in it, in a union of enjoyment, I knew not what to say, having never read or heard of such an experience. I dreaded delusion and feared that all was not right, for I had known nothing of the operations of God in souls. I had only read Francis de Sales, Thomas a' Kempis, The Spiritual Combat, and the Holy Scriptures. I was a stranger to those interior and spiritual books where such states are described.

All amusements appeared dull and insipid. I wondered how I had ever enjoyed them. I could find no enjoyment out of God, although sometimes unfaithful enough to endeavor it. I was not astonished that martyrs gave their lives for Christ. I thought them happy, and sighed after their privilege of suffering for Him; for I so esteemed the cross, that my greatest trouble was want of suffering as much as my heart thirsted for.

This esteem for the cross continually increased, and though afterwards I lost the sensible enjoyment thereof, yet the love no more left me than the cross itself. Indeed, it has ever been my faithful companion, changing and augmenting, in proportion to the changes and dispositions of my inward state. So eager was I for the cross, that I endeavored to make myself feel the utmost rigor of every mortification. Yet this only increased my desire to suffer. God alone can prepare crosses suitable to a soul that thirsts for a following of His sufferings and a conformity to His death. The more my state of prayer augmented, my desire of suffering grew stronger, as the full weight of heavy crosses from every side came thundering upon me.

The peculiar property of this prayer of the heart is to give a strong faith. Mine was without limits, as was also my resignation to God, and my confidence in Him, my love of His will, and of the order of His providence over me. I was timorous before, now feared nothing. In such a case one feels the efficacy of the words: "My yoke is easy, and my burden is light" (Matt. xi. 30).

I had a secret desire from that time to be wholly devoted to the disposal of my God, let that be what it would. I said: "What couldst Thou demand of me that I would not willingly offer Thee? Oh, spare me not." The cross and humiliations were represented to my mind in the most frightful colors,—but this deterred me not. I yielded myself up as a willing victim, and our Lord seemed to accept of my sacrifice, for His divine providence furnished me incessantly with opportunities for putting it to the test.

I could scarce hear God spoken of without being almost transported out of myself. What surprised me most was the great difficulty I had to say vocal prayers. As soon as I opened my lips, the love of God seized me so strongly, I was swallowed up in a profound silence and an inexpressible peace. I made fresh attempts, but still in vain. There was made in me, without the sound of words, a continual prayer, which seemed to me to be the prayer of Christ Himself; a prayer of the Word, made by the Spirit, that asketh for us that which is good, perfect, and conformable to the will of God (Rom. viii. 26, 27).

My domestic crosses continued. I was prevented from seeing or writing to Mrs. Granger. Going to divine service or the blessed sacrament were woeful offences; and the only amusement I had left me was visiting the sick poor, and performing the lowest offices for them.

But now my prayer-time began to be exceedingly distressing. I compelled myself to continue at it, though deprived of all comfort; and yet when I was not employed therein, I felt an ardent longing for it. I suffered inexpressible anguish, and endeavored with the severest inflictions of corporeal austerities to mitigate and divert it—but in vain; the dryness and barrenness still increased; I found no more that enlivening vigor which had carried me on with great swiftness. My passions (not thoroughly mortified) revived, and caused me new conflicts. I relapsed into a vain complacency and fondness for myself. My propensity to pride and vanity, which seemed quite dead, while I was so filled with the love of God, now showed itself again, and gave me severe exercise; which made me lament the exterior beauty of my person, and pray to God incessantly that He would remove from me that obstacle, and make me ugly. I could have wished to be deaf, blind and dumb, that nothing might divert me from my love of God.

I set out on a journey we had to make, and appeared like those lamps which emit a new flash, when just on the point of extinguishing. Alas! how many snares were laid in my way at every step! I even committed infidelities through unwatchfulness. But, O my Lord, with what rigor didst Thou punish them! A useless glance was checked as a sin. How many tears did those faults cost me which I fell into, through a weak compliance, and even against my will! How often didst Thou make me sensible of Thy love towards me, notwithstanding my blemishes.

O sinner! hast thou any reason to complain of God? Admit it is owing to thyself if thou goest wrong; that in departing from Him thou disobeyest His call; and that, after all this, when thou returnest, He is ready to receive thee.

When I was at Paris, and the clergy saw me so young, they appeared astonished. Those to whom I opened my state told me that I could never enough thank God for the graces conferred on me; that if I knew them I should be amazed; and if I were not faithful, I should be most ungrateful. Some declared they never knew any woman whom God held so closely, and in so great a purity of conscience. I believe what rendered it so was the continual care Thou hadst over me, O my God. I became deeply assured of what the prophet hath said: "Except the Lord keep the city, the watchman waketh but in vain " (Psa. cxxvii. 1). Thou, O my Love, wast my faithful keeper, who didst defend my heart against all enemies, preventing the least faults, or correcting them when vivacity had occasioned their being committed. But alas! my dear Love, when Thou didst cease to watch for me, or left me to myself, how weak was I, and how easily did my enemies prevail over me! Let others ascribe their victory to their own fidelity. I shall never attribute them to anything else than Thy paternal care over me. To Thee only I owe everything, O my Deliverer; and being indebted to Thee gives me infinite joy.

While at Paris, I relaxed in my usual exercises, on account of the little time I had, and the dryness and distress which had seized my heart, the hand which sustained me being hid, and my Beloved withdrawn. I fell into other faults, as having my neck a little too bare, though not near so much as others. I wept bitterly because I was remiss; and that was my torment. I sought all about for Him who had inflamed my heart. I inquired for tidings of Him. But, alas! hardly anybody knew Him. I cried: "Oh, Thou Best Beloved of my soul, hadst Thou been near me these disasters had not befallen me. Tell me where Thou feedest, where Thou makest Thy flock to rest at noon?" I say that I spoke thus to Him. In reality, it all passed almost in silence, for could not speak. My heart had a language which was carried on without the sound of words, understood of its Beloved. Oh, sacred language, of which experience only gives the comprehension! Let not any think it a barren language, and the effect of imagination. Far different,—it is the silent expression of the Word in the soul. As He never ceases to speak, so He never ceases to operate. If people once come to know the operations of the Lord, in souls wholly resigned to His guiding, it would fill them with admiration and awe.

As I saw that the purity of my state was like to be sullied by too great commerce with the creatures, I made haste to finish what had detained me at Paris, to return to the country. The pain I felt after my faults was inexpressible. It was not an anguish that arose from any distinct conception, from any particular affection; but a devouring fire which ceased not till the fault was consumed and the soul purified by it. It was a banishment of my soul from the presence of its Beloved, its Bridegroom. I could have no access to Him, neither could I have any rest out of Him. I knew not what to do. I was like the dove out of the ark, which, finding no rest for the sole of her foot, was constrained to return to the ark; but, finding the window shut, could only fly about it.

One day, I went to take a walk at a public park, from excess of vanity to show myself. Oh, my Lord, how didst Thou make me sensible of this fault? But far from punishing me in letting me partake of the amusement, Thou didst it in holding me so close to Thyself, that I could give no attention to anything but my fault and Thy displeasure. After this I was invited to an entertainment at St. Cloud. Through vanity and weak compliance, I went. The affair was magnificent; they could relish it, but I was filled with bitterness. I could eat nothing, enjoy nothing: my disquiet appeared on my countenance. Oh, what tears did it cost me! For above three months my Beloved withdrew His favoring presence, and I could see nothing but an angry God.

I was on this occasion, and in another journey which I took with my husband into Touraine, like those animals destined for slaughter, which on certain days they adorn with greens and flowers, and bring in pomp into the city, before they kill them. This weak beauty, on the eve of its decline, shone forth with new brightness, in order to become the sooner extinct. I was shortly after sorely afflicted with small-pox.

One day as I walked to church, followed by a footman, in crossing a bridge I met a poor man; I went to give him alms; he thanked me but refused them, and then spoke in a wonderful manner of God; he displayed to me my whole heart, my love to God, my charity, my too great fondness for my beauty, and all my faults. He told me the Lord required of me the utmost purity and height of perfection. My heart assented to his reproofs. I heard him with silence and respect. His words penetrated my soul. When I arrived at the church I fainted; but have never seen the man since.

CHAPTER IX.

After this, my husband enjoying some intermission of his ailments, had a mind to go to Orleans, and from thence to Touraine. In this journey my vanity made its last blaze. I received abundance of visits and applause. How clearly did I see the folly of men who are so taken with vain beauty! I disliked the passion, yet not that in myself which caused it, though I sometimes ardently desired to be delivered from it. The continual combat of nature and grace cost me no small affliction.

What augmented the temptation was, that they esteemed in me virtue, joined with youth and beauty; not knowing that all the virtue was only in God, and His protection, and all the weakness in myself.

The heinousness of sins is measured by the state of the person who commits them; the least unfaithfulness in a spouse is more injurious to her husband than far greater ones in his domestics.

We met with accidents in this journey, sufficient to have terrified anyone; yet my resignation to God was so strong, I was fearless, even where there was apparently no possibility for escape. At one time in a narrow pass, we did not perceive, until too far advanced to draw back, the road was undermined by the river Loire, which ran beneath, and the banks had fallen in; so that in places the footmen were obliged to support one side of the carriage. All were terrified, yet God kept me tranquil; and I rejoiced at the prospect of losing my life by a singular stroke of His providence.

On my return, I went to see Mrs. Granger. She

encouraged me to pursue my first design, and advised me to cover my neck entirely, which I have ever since, notwithstanding the singularity of it.

I besought my God to deprive me of power to displease Him, and cried: "Art Thou not strong enough wholly to eradicate duplicity out of my heart?" For my vanity broke forth when occasions offered; yet I quickly returned to God, and He received me with open arms, and gave me fresh testimonials of His love, which filled me with the most painful reflections on my offence; for though wretched vanity was still so prevalent, yet my love to God was such, that after my wanderings, I would rather have chosen His rod than His caresses. His interests were more dear to me than my own, and I wished He would have done Himself justice upon me.

If anyone reads this life with attention, he will see on God's part nothing but goodness, mercy, and love, and on my part nothing but weakness, sin and infidelity. If there be anything that is good, it is Thine, O my God! I have nothing to glory in but infirmities and unworthiness. In that everlasting marriage-union Thou hast made with me, I brought with me nothing but weakness, sin and misery. Oh, my Love! how I rejoice to owe all to Thee, and that Thou favorest my heart with a sight of the treasures and riches of Thy grace and love! Thou hast dealt by me, as if a magnificent king should marry a poor slave, forget her slavery, give her all the ornaments which render her pleasing in his eyes, and freely pardon all her faults, ill qualities, ignorance and bad education. This Thou hast made my case. My poverty is become my riches, and in my weakness I have found strength. Oh, if any knew, with what confusion the indulgent favors of God cover the soul after its faults!—'t is inconceivable! Such a soul would wish with all its power to satisfy the Divine justice.

On my arrival home, I found my husband taken with the gout; my little daughter ill, and like to die of small-pox; my eldest son, too, took it, and of so malignant a type, it rendered him as disfigured as before he was beautiful. I had no doubt but I should take the small-pox. Mrs. Granger advised me to leave. My father offered to take me home, with my second son, whom I tenderly loved. But my mother-in-law would not suffer it. She persuaded my husband it was useless, and sent for a physician, who seconded her in it, saying I should as readily take it at a distance as here. She proved a Jephtha, and sacrificed us both, though innocently. Had she known what followed, she would have acted otherwise. All the town was stirred. Everyone begged her to send me away, and cried out it was cruel to expose me. They set upon me, too, imagining I was unwilling to go; for I had not told that she was so averse to it. I had no other disposition than to sacrifice myself to Divine Providence; and though I might have removed, notwithstanding my mother-in-law's resistance, yet I would not without her consent. Oh, divine will of my Lord! Thou wast my only life, in the midst of all my miseries.

I continued in this spirit of sacrifice to God, waiting in entire resignation, for whatever He should be pleased to ordain. I cannot express what nature suffered; I was like one who sees both certain death and an easy remedy, without being able to avoid the former or try the latter. I had no less apprehension for my younger son than for myself. My mother-in-law so excessively doted on the eldest, the rest of us were indifferent to her. Yet if she had known that the younger would have died of the small-pox, she would not have acted as she did. God makes use of creatures and their natural inclinations to accomplish His designs. When I see in the creatures a conduct unreasonable and mortifying, I mount higher, and look upon them as instruments both of the mercy and justice of God; for His justice is full of mercy.

When I told my husband I was sick, and taking the small-pox, he said it was only imagination. I let Mrs. Granger know. She was affected by the treatment I met with, and encouraged me to offer myself to the Lord. At length I was seized with a great shivering and pain. They would not yet believe I was sick; but in a few hours they thought my life in danger; for I was also taken with inflammation on my lungs. My mother-in-law's favorite physician was not in town, nor the resident surgeon. So little attendance was paid me, I was on the point of death. My husband, not being able to see me, left me entirely to his mother. She would not allow any physician but her own to prescribe for me, yet did not send for him, though he was within a day's journey of us. I opened not my mouth to request any succor. The peace I enjoyed within, on account of that perfect resignation, in which God kept me by His grace, was so great it made me forget myself, in the midst of such violent and oppressive disorders.

But the Lord's protection was indeed wonderful. It pleased Him so to order it, that a skillful surgeon, who had attended me before, passing by our house, inquired after me. They told him I was extremely ill. He alighted immediately, and came in to see me. Never was a man more surprised, when he saw the frightful condition I was in. The small-pox, which could not come out, had fallen on my nose with such force that it was quite black. He thought there had been a gangrene in it, and that it was going to fall off. My eyes were like two coals; but I was not alarmed; for at that time I could have made a sacrifice of all things, and was pleased that God should avenge Himself on that face, which had betrayed me into so many infidelities.

I am more particular in this relation, to show how advantageous it is to resign one's self to God without reserve. Though in appearance He leaves us for a time to prove and exercise our faith, He never fails us, when our need of Him is the more pressing.

The malady fell into my eyes, and inflamed them with such severe pain, that I thought I should lose them. I had those violent pains for three weeks, during which I got little sleep. I could not shut my eyes, they were so full of the small-pox, nor open them by reason of the pain I endured. There was the greatest probability that I should lose my sight, but I was wholly reconciled. My throat, palate, and gums were likewise so filled with the pock, that I could not take any nourishment, without suffering extremely. My whole body looked like that of a leper. All that saw me said, they had never seen such a shocking spectacle. But my soul was kept in a contentment not to be expressed. I would not have changed my condition for that of the most happy prince in the world.

Everyone thought I would be inconsolable; and several expressed their sympathy in my sad condition, while I lay still, in the secret fruition of a joy unspeakable, in this total deprivation of what had been a snare to my pride, and to the passions of men. I praised God in profound silence. None ever heard any complaints from me, because of pain or the loss of my beauty. I rejoiced at, and was exceedingly thankful for the interior liberty I gained thereby; and they construed this as a great crime.

My youngest boy took the distemper the same day with myself, and died for want of care. This blow indeed struck me to the heart, yet the spirit of sacrifice possessed me so strongly, that, though I loved this child tenderly, I never shed a tear at hearing of his death. The day he was buried, the doctor said my little girl could not survive him two days. My eldest son was not yet out of danger, so I saw myself stripped of all my children at once, my husband indisposed, and myself extremely ill. My little girl lived some years.

After my eldest son was better, he came into my chamber. I was surprised at the extraordinary change I saw in him. His face, lately so fair and beautiful, was like a coarse spot of earth, full of furrows. That gave me the curiosity to view myself in the glass. I felt shocked; God had ordered the sacrifice in all its reality.

Some things now fell out by the contrariety of my mother-in-law, that caused me severe crosses, and put the finishing stroke to my son's face. However, my heart was firm in God, and strengthened itself by the number and greatness of my sufferings. I was as a victim incessantly offered upon the altar, to HIM who first sacrificed Himself for love.

They sent me pomatums to recover my complexion, and fill up the hollows of the small-pox. I had seen wonderful effects on others, and had a mind to try them. But love, jealous of His work, would not suffer it. A voice in my heart said, "If I would have had thee fair, I would have left thee as thou wert." I was obliged to lay aside every remedy, and to go into the air, which made the pitting worse; and to expose myself in the street to the eyes of everyone, when the redness of the small-pox was at the worst, in order to make my humiliation triumph, where I had exalted my pride.

My husband kept his bed almost all that time. As he lost that which before gave him so much pleasure in viewing me, he grew more susceptible of impressions against me. The persons who spoke to him to my disadvantage, finding themselves better hearkened to, spoke more boldly and frequently. There was only Thou, O my God, who changed not for me. Thou didst redouble my interior graces, in proportion as Thou didst augment my exterior crosses.

CHAPTER X.

My waiting maid became every day more haughty. Seeing her scoldings did not now torment me, she thought, if she could hinder me from going to the communion, she would give me the greatest of vexations. She was not mistaken, O Divine One, since the only satisfaction of my life was to receive and honor Thee. When she discovered me going thither, she ran to tell my mother-in-law and my husband. Their invectives lasted the whole day. If a word escaped me in my own justification, it was enough to make them raise an outcry against all devotion. If I made them no answer at all, they still said the most grating things. If I fell sick, they took occasion to come to quarrel with me in my bed, saying my communion and prayers made me sick; as if there had been nothing else could make me ill but my devotion to Thee, O my Beloved!

I had scarcely any rest but what I found in the love of Thy will, O my God, and submission to Thy orders, however rigorous. They incessantly watched my words and actions, to find occasion against me. They chided me all the day long, continually repeating and harping over the same things, even before the servants. How often have I made my meals on my tears, which were interpreted as the most criminal in the world! If I recited anything I heard, they would render me accountable for the truth of it. If I kept silence, they taxed me with perverseness; if I knew anything without telling it, that was a crime; if I told it, they said I forged it. Sometimes they tormented me for days successively, without giving me any relaxation. The girls said: "Feign sickness, and get a little rest." I made no reply. The love of God so possessed me, it would not allow me to seek relief by a single word or look. Sometimes I said: "Oh, that I had but any one to whom I might unbosom myself, what a relief it would be!" But it was not granted me.

Yet, if I happened to be for some days freed from the exterior cross, it was a sensible distress and a punishment more difficult to bear than the severest trials. I then comprehended what Teresa says, "Let me suffer or die." For this absence of the cross was so grievous to me that I languished with the ardency of desire for its return. But no sooner was this earnest longing granted, and the blessed cross returned again than, strange as it may seem, it appeared so weighty as to be almost insupportable.

Though I loved my father extremely, and he loved me tenderly, I never spoke of my sufferings. One of my relations, who loved me much, told my father of them. Soon after, I went to see my father, who, contrary to his custom, sharply reprimanded me for suffering them to treat me in such a manner, without saying anything in my own defence. I answered that, if they knew what my husband said to me, that was confusion enough for me, without my bringing any more of it on myself by replies; that if they did not notice it, I ought not to cause it to be observed, nor expose my husband's weakness; that remaining silent stopped all disputes, whereas I might cause them to be continued and increased by my replies. My father answered that I should continue to act as God should inspire me, and never spoke to me of it any more.

They were ever talking to me against my father, whom I tenderly loved, against my relations, and all I esteemed. I felt this more keenly than all they said. I could not forbear defending them, and therein I did wrong, as whatever I said served only to provoke them.

No matter what they said against me, love would not allow me to justify myself. I spoke not to my husband of what my mother-in-law or the girl did to me, except the first year, when I was not sufficiently touched with the power of God to suffer such treatment. Nay, I did more, for as my mother-in-law and husband were both passionate, they often quarreled. Then I was in favor, and to me they made mutual complaint. I never told the one what the other said. And though it might have been of service to me, humanly speaking, to take advantage of such opportunities, I never made use of them to complain of either. I did not rest till I had reconciled them. I spoke many obliging things of the one to the other, which always made them friends again; though I knew I should pay dear for their reunion. For scarcely were they reconciled, but they joined together against me.

All my crosses would have seemed little, if I might have had liberty to pray and be alone. But I was obliged still to continue in their presence, with such subjection as is scarcely conceivable. My husband looked at his watch, if I had liberty allowed me for prayer, to see if I stayed above half an hour. If I exceeded it, he grew uneasy. Sometimes I said to him: "Grant me one hour to divert and employ myself as I have a mind." Though he would have granted it to me for other diversions, yet for prayer he would not. Inexperience caused me much trouble, and I have often given occasion for what they made me suffer. For ought I not to have looked on my captivity as an effect of the will of my God, to content myself therein, and to make it my only desire and prayer? But I often fell back again into the anxiety of wishing to get time for prayer, which was not agreeable to my husband. Those faults were more frequent in the beginning. Afterwards I prayed to God in His own retreat, in the temple of my heart, and then I went out no more.

We went into the country, where I committed many faults, letting myself go too much after my inward attraction. I thought I might do it then because my husband diverted himself with building. If I stayed from him he was dissatisfied, which sometimes happened, as he was continually talking with the workmen. I set myself in a corner, and there had my work with me, but could scarcely do anything by reason of the attraction which made the work fall out of my hands. I passed hours this way, without being able either to open my eyes or know what passed in me, but I had nothing to wish for, nor yet be afraid of. Everywhere I found my proper centre, because everywhere I found God.

As we had not yet built the chapel, and were far from any church, I could not go to prayers or sacrament, without the permission of my husband—and he was reluctant to suffer me, except Sundays and holidays. I could not go out in the coach, so that I was obliged to get to service early in the morning, to which, feeble as I was, I made an effort to creep on foot, though it was a quarter of a league distant. And God wrought wonders for me; for generally, in the morning when I went to prayers, my husband did not wake till after I returned. Often, as I was going out, the weather was so cloudy, that the girl I took with me told me I could not go; or, I should be soaked with the rain. I answered her with my usual confidence: "God will assist us." I generally reached the chapel without being wet. While there the rain fell excessively. When I returned it ceased. When I got home it began again with fresh violence.

I often suddenly was seized with a strong impulse to go to prayers. My maid would say: "But, madam, you are going to tire yourself in vain. There will be no service." However, I went full of faith, and at my arrival have found them just ready to begin. When I wanted to hear from, or write to Mother Granger, I often felt a strong propensity to go to the door. There I found a messenger with a letter from her, which could not have fallen into my hands but for that.

One day when they thought I was going to see my father, I ran off to Mother Granger. It was discovered, and cost me such crosses as I can not express. Their rage against me was so excessive, it would be incredible. Even my writing to her was extremely difficult. For as I had the utmost abhorrence of a lie, I forbade the footman to tell any. My husband and mother-in-law were always inveighing against Mother Granger, though in reality they esteemed her.

The most sensible cross to me now was the revolting of my own son against me, whom they inspired with so great a contempt for me, that I could not bear to see him without extreme affliction. When I was in my chamber with some of my friends, they sent him to listen to what we said, and as he saw this pleased them, he invented a hundred things to tell them. What gave me the severest pang was the loss of my child. If I caught him in a lie, he would upbraid me, saying: "My grandmother says you have been a greater liar than I." I answered him: "Therefore I know the deformity of that vice, and how hard a thing it is to get the better of it; and for this reason, I would not have you suffer the like." He spoke things very offensive, and because he saw the awe I stood in of his grandmother and his father, if in their absence I found fault with him for anything, he insultingly upbraided me, and said I wanted to set up for his mistress, because they were not there. All this they approved of. One day he went to see my father, and rashly began talking against me to him, as he was used to his grandmother. But it did not meet with the same recompense. It affected my father to tears. He came to our house to desire he might be corrected for it. They promised it should be done, yet never did it. I was grievously afraid of the consequences of so bad an education. I told Mother Granger, who consoled me, and said that since I could not remedy it, I must suffer and leave everything to God; and that this child would be my cross.

Another great cross was the difficulty I had in attending my husband. He was displeased when I was not with him; yet when I was with him, he never expressed any pleasure in it, nor at anything I did. When he was in a good humor, and I was carrying something agreeable to him, then my mother-in-law would snatch it out of my hands, and carry it herself. And as he thought I was not so studious to please him, he would fly in a rage against me, and express great thankfulness to his mother. I silently suffered it all. I used all my skill to gain my mother-in-law's favor, but could not succeed. How bitter and grievous, O my God, would such a life be were it not for Thee? But Thou hast sweetened and reconciled it to me.

CHAPTER XI.

About nine months after my recovery from small-pox, Father LaCombe brought me a letter from Father de la Motte, recommending him to my esteem. I was loth to make new acquaintances, but the fear of offending prevailed. After a short conversation we both desired a further opportunity. God had already made use of me for the conversion of three of his order. The strong desire he had of seeing me again induced him to come to our country house.

A way opened for me to speak to him. As he was with my husband, who relished his company, he was taken ill, and retired to the garden. My husband bade me see what was the matter with him. He told me he had remarked in my countenance a deep presence of God, which had given him a strong desire of seeing me again. God assisted me to open to him the interior path of the soul, and conveyed so much grace to him through this poor channel, that he went away changed into quite another man.

My disposition was a continual prayer, without knowing it to be such; for the presence of God was so plentifully given, that it seemed to be more in me than my very self. The sensibility was so powerful, so penetrating, it seemed irresistible; and love took from me all liberty of my own. At other times I was so dry, I felt nothing but the pain of absence, which was the keener, as the Divine presence had before been so sensible. When love was present, I forgot all my troubles and pains. It appeared to me as if I had never experienced any. It seemed as if it would never return again. I still thought it was through some fault of mine it was withdrawn, and that rendered me inconsolable. Had I known it had been a state through which it was necessary to pass, I should not have been troubled; for my strong love to the will of God would have rendered everything easy; the property of this prayer being to give a great love to the order of God, with so sublime and perfect a reliance on Him, as to fear nothing, whether danger, thunders, spirits, or death. It gives a great abstraction from one's own interests and reputation; all being swallowed up in the esteem of the will of God.

At home, I was accused of everything that was spoiled or broken. At first I told the truth, and said it was not I. They persisted, and accused me of lying. I then made no reply. They told all their tales to such as came to the house. But when I was afterwards alone with the same persons, I never undeceived them. My heart kept its habitation in the tacit consciousness of my own innocence, not concerning myself whether they thought well or ill of me; excluding all the world, all opinions or censures, and minding nothing but the friendship of God only.

If through infidelity I tried at any time to justify myself, I always failed, and drew upon myself new crosses, both within and without. But I was so enamored with it, the greatest cross of all would have been to be without any. When the cross was taken from me for any short space, it seemed to me that it was because of the bad use I made of it; and that my unfaithfulness deprived me of so great an advantage, for I never knew its value better than in its loss. Oh, dear cross, my faithful companion! O my Love, I cried, punish me any way, but take not the cross from me. This amiable cross returned to me with so much the more weight, as my desire was more vehement. I could not reconcile two things, to desire the cross with so much ardor, and support it with so much difficulty and pain.

God knows how to render the crosses conformable to the ability of the creature to bear them; giving them always something new and unexpected. Hereby my soul began to be more resigned, and to comprehend that the state of absence, and of wanting what I longed for, was in its turn more profitable than that of always abounding, because this latter nourished **self-love.** If God did not act thus, the soul would never die to itself. Self-love is so crafty and dangerous, it cleaves to everything.

In acts of charity I was assiduous. So great was my tenderness for the poor, that I wished to supply all their wants. I could not see their necessity, without reproaching myself for the plenty I enjoyed. I deprived myself of all I could to help them. The best at my table was distributed among them. Being refused by others, they all came to me. "Oh, my divine Love," I cried, "it is Thy substance; I am only the steward. I ought to distribute it according to Thy will." I found means to relieve them without letting myself be known, because I had one who dispensed my alms privately. I caused young girls to be taught how to earn their livelihood, especially such as were handsome; that, being employed and having whereon to live, they might not be tempted to throw themselves away. God used me to reclaim several from their disorderly lives. I went to visit the sick, to comfort them, to make their beds. I made ointments, dressed their wounds, buried their dead. I furnished tradesmen and mechanics wherewith to keep up their shops. My heart was much opened toward my fellow-creatures in distress; and few could carry charity much farther than our Lord enabled me to do, both while married and since.

To purify me from the mixture I might make of His gifts with my own self-love, He gave me interior probations, which were heavy. I began to experience an insupportable weight, in that piety which had formerly been so easy and delightful; not that I did not love it, but I found myself defective in that noble practice of it, to which I aspired. The more I loved it, the more I labored to acquire what I failed in. But, alas! I seemed continually to be overcome by that which was contrary to it. My heart was detached from all sensual pleasures. I do things as if I did them not. If I eat, or refresh myself, it is with an entire mortification of the keenness of sensation in all the natural functions.

The small-pox so hurt one of my eyes, it was feared I would lose it. The gland at the corner of my eye was much injured. An imposthume arose from time to time between the nose and the eye, which gave me severe pain till lanced. It swelled all my head. I could not bear even a pillow. The least noise was agony, though sometimes they made a great commotion in my chamber. Yet this was a precious time to me, for I was left alone, without interruption; and it answered the desire I had for suffering, a desire so great, that all the austerities of the body were but as a drop of water to quench so great a fire. Thou alone, O crucified Saviour, canst make the cross truly effectual for the death of self. Let others bless themselves in ease or gaiety, grandeur or pleasure, my desires were all turned to the silent path of suffering for Christ, and to be united to Him, through the mortification of all that was of nature in me, that my senses, appetites and will, dead to these, might wholly live in Him.

I obtained leave to go to Paris for the cure of my eye; yet much more through the desire to see Monsieur Bertot, a man of profound experience, Mother Granger had assigned to me for my director. I went to take leave of my father, who embraced me with peculiar tenderness, little thinking it would be our last adieu.

Paris was a place no longer to be dreaded. The throngs only served to draw me into a deep recollection, and the noise of the streets but augmented my inward prayer.

I went to pass ten days at an abbey four leagues from Paris, the abbess of which had a particular friendship for me. Here my union with God seemed more close and intimate.

One day I awoke at four in the morning, with a strong impression that my father was dead; and though my soul was in great contentment, yet my love for him affected it with sorrow, and my body with weakness. Under the daily troubles which befell me, my will was so subservient to Thine, O my God, it appeared absolutely united to it. There seemed to be no will left in me but Thine. If I had a will, it was in union with Thine, as two well tuned lutes in concert are one pure harmony. This union of the will establishes in perfect peace. Yet, though my own will was lost, as to its operations, I have found since, in the strange states I have been through, how much it had yet to cost me to have it totally lost, as to all its properties in all the circumstances, and whole extent thereof, so that the soul should retain no more any interest or desire of its own, of either time or eternity, but only the interest of God in the manner known to Himself, not in our way of conceiving. How many think their own wills quite lost, while they are yet far from it! They would find they still subsist, if they met with severe trials. Who is there who does not wish something for himself, either of interest, wealth, honor, pleasure, conveniency or liberty? And he who thinks his mind loose from all these objects, because he possesses them, might soon perceive his attachment to them, were he stripped. If there are found in a whole age three persons so dead to everything, as to be utterly resigned to Providence without any exception, they may well pass for prodigies of grace.

In the afternoon as I was with the abbess, I told her I had strong presentiments of my father's death. I could hardly speak, I was so affected within, and enfeebled without. Presently one came from my husband to inform me my father was ill. I said: "He is dead, I have not a doubt about it." I sent to Paris immediately, to hire a coach, to go the sooner; mine waited for me at the midway. I went at nine o'clock at night. They said I was going to destroy myself, for I had no acquaintance with me, as I had sent my maid to Paris, and being in a religious house, I had no footman. The abbess told me, since I thought my father dead, it would be rash in me to expose myself, and run the risk of my life; that coaches could hardly pass the way I was going, it being no beaten road. I answered it was my duty to go to my father, and I ought not, on a bare apprehension, to exempt myself from it. I went alone, abandoned to Providence, with people unknown. My weakness was so great, I could hardly keep my seat in the coach, yet I was forced to alight, on account of dangerous places in the road.

I was obliged, about midnight, to cross a forest, notorious for murders and robberies. The most intrepid dreaded it; but my resignation left me scarce any room to think about it. Oh, what fears and uneasiness does a resigned soul spare itself!

I found on my arrival, that my father was already buried, on account of the excessive heat. It was ten o'clock at night. All wore the habit of mourning. I had travelled thirty leagues in a day and night. As I was weak, not having taken any nourishment, I was put to bed.

About two in the morning my husband got up, and having gone out of my chamber, returned presently, crying out: "My daughter is dead!" She was my only daughter, dearly beloved, truly lovely. She had so many graces both of body and mind, one must have been insensible not to have loved her. She had an extraordinary love to God. Often was she found in corners at prayer. As soon as she perceived me at prayer, she came and joined; and if she discovered I had been without her, she would weep and cry, "Ah, mamma, you pray, but I do n't." When we were alone and she saw my eyes closed, she'd whisper, "Are you asleep?" and then cry out, "Ah, no, you are praying to our Jesus;" and dropping on her knees, would begin to pray too. She was several times whipped by her grandmother, because she said she would never have any other husband but our Lord, yet she could never make her say otherwise. She was innocent, modest, dutiful, endearing, and beautiful. Her father doted on her, and to me she was dear more for the qualities of her mind than her beautiful person. She was my consolation; for she had as much affection for me, as her brother had aversion. She died of an unseasonable bleeding.

There remained to me only the son of my sorrow. He fell ill to the point of death, but was restored at the prayer of Mother Granger, now my only consolation after God. I no more wept for my child than for my father. Both died in July, 1672. From henceforth crosses were not spared me, yet they were only the shadows of those I have since passed through, pursuant to a marriage contract which I had lately entered into with Christ. In this spiritual marriage I claimed for my dowry only crosses, scourges, persecutions, ignominies, lowliness, and nothingness of self, which in His great goodness, and for wise ends, He has been pleased to grant me.

One day, in great distress on account of the redoubling of outward and inward crosses, I went into my closet to vent my grief. M. Bertot was brought to my mind, with this wish: "Oh, that he was sensible of what I suffer!" Though he wrote seldom, and with great difficulty, yet he wrote me a letter dated the same day about the cross, the most consolatory he ever wrote on that subject. Sometimes my spirit was so oppressed with continued crosses, that when alone my eyes turned every way, to see if they could find anything to give relief. A word, a sigh, a trifle, to know that anyone took part in my grief, would have been some comfort; but that was not granted me, not even to look toward heaven, or make any complaint. Love held me then so closely, that it would have this miserable nature to perish without giving it any nourishment.

CHAPTER XII.

A lady of rank, whom I visited, took a particular liking to me. This lady began to be touched with the sense of God. Wanting once to take me to the play, I refused to go. Insisting to know my sentiment of plays, I told her I entirely disapproved of them, especially for a Christian. What I said made such an impression, she never went again.

Being once with her and another lady, who was fond of talking and who had read the fathers, they spoke much of God. This lady spoke learnedly of Him. I said scarcely anything, being drawn to silence. My acquaintance came next day to see me, and said: "Your silence had something in it which penetrated to the bottom of my soul; and I could not relish what the other said." Then we spoke to one another with open hearts. God left indelible impressions of His grace on her soul, and she continued so athirst for Him, she could scarcely endure to converse on any other subject. That she might become wholly His, He visited her with such severe crosses, and poured His grace so abundantly into her heart, that He soon became sole Master. After the death of her husband, and the loss of most of her fortune, she went to reside four leagues from our house, on a small estate she had left. She obtained my husband's consent to my spending a week with her, to console her. God gave her all she wanted. She was surprised at my expressing things to her so far above my natural capacity. But God gave me the gift for her sake, diffusing a flood of grace into her soul, without regarding the unworthiness of the channel He was pleased to use. Since that time her soul has been the temple of the Holy Spirit, and our hearts indissolubly united.

My husband and I took a journey together, in which my resignation and humility were exercised. We all liked to have perished in a river. The rest in a desperate fright threw themselves out of the coach, which sunk in the moving sand. I continued so inwardly occupied, I did not once think of the danger. God delivered me from it without my thought of avoiding it.

As my husband's maladies daily increased, he resolved to go to St. Reine. He desired none but me with him, and told me: "If they never spoke to me against you, I should be more easy, and you more happy." In this journey I committed many faults of self-love and self-seeking; and experienced what I should be without Thy Fatherly care, O Lord. For some time past, Thou hadst withdrawn from me that sweet interior correspondence which before I had only to follow. I was like a poor traveller lost in the night, and could find no way, path, or track. My husband, in his return from St. Reine, passed by St. Edm. Having now no children but my first-born son, who was often at the gates of death, he wished exceedingly for heirs, and prayed for them earnestly. God granted his desire, and gave me a second son. As I was several weeks without any one daring to speak to me, on account of my great weakness, it was a time of retreat and silence. God took a new possession of me. It was a time of continual joy. As I had experienced many inward difficulties, weaknesses, and withdrawings of my Love, it was a new life. I was in the fruition of beatitude. It was preparative to a total privation of comfort for several years, which began with the death of Mrs. Granger, who had been my only consolation under God. Before my return from St. Reine I heard she was dead.

It was the most afflicting stroke I had ever felt. I thought, had I been with her at her death, I might have received her last instructions, but God so ordered it that I was deprived of her assistance in almost all my losses, in order to render the strokes more painful.

My brother now openly showed his hatred. He married at Orleans, and my husband had the complaisance to go to his marriage, though he was in a poor state of health, the roads bad, and so covered over with snow, that we had like to have been upset many times. Yet, far from appearing obliged by his politeness, my brother quarrelled with him more than ever, without any reason, and I was the butt of both their resentments.

On my return, my brother treated me with utmost contempt. Yet, my mind was so fully drawn inward, that though we had much more danger on the road than in going, I had no thought about myself, but all about my husband; so that seeing the coach overturning, I said: "Fear not, it is on my side that it falls; it will not hurt you." I believe, had all perished, I should not have been moved. My peace was so profound nothing could shake it. If these times continued, we should be too strong. They now began to come but seldom, and were followed with long and wearisome privations. Since that time my brother has turned on the side of God, but not to me. It has been by particular permission of God, and the conduct of His providence that caused him and other religious persons, who have persecuted me, to think they were rendering glory to God, and doing acts of justice.

After this there fell out a perplexing affair. To me

it caused great crosses, and seemed designed for nothing else. A person conceived so much malice against my husband, he was determined to ruin him by entering into a private engagement with my brother, by which he obtained power to demand, in the name of the king's brother, two hundred thousand livres, which he pretended my brother and I owed him. My brother signed the processes, upon an assurance that he should not pay anything. I think he did not understand. This affair so chagrined my husband, that it shortened his days. He was so angry with me, though I was innocent, that he could not speak but in a fury. He would give me no light into the affair. In the height of his rage, he said he would not meddle with it, but give me my portion, and let me live as I could; with many other things still more grating. My brother would not suffer anything to be done. The day the trial was to come on, after prayer, I felt strongly pressed to go to the judges. I was wonderfully assisted to discover and unravel all the turns and artifices of this affair, without knowing how I could have been able to do it. The first judge was so surprised to see the affair so different from what he had thought it before, that he himself exhorted me to go to the other judges. God enabled me to manifest the truth in so clear a light they saw the falsehood of every point. They would have condemned the plaintiff to pay the costs, if he had not been so great a prince, who lent his name to the scheme. To save the honor of the prince, they ordered us to pay him fifty crowns. Hereby the two hundred thousand livres were reduced to one hundred and fifty. My husband was exceedingly pleased at what I had done; but my brother appeared as outrageous against me, as if I had caused him some great loss.

Thus ended an affair, which appeared so weighty and alarming.

I fell into a state of total privation which lasted nearly seven years. I seemed cast down from a throne of enjoyment, like Nebuchadnezzar, to live among beasts; a deplorable state, yet of great advantage to me, by the use Divine wisdom made of it. This state of emptiness, darkness, and impotency, went far beyond any trials I had ever met. God gives what is best, not what we most relish. Were people convinced of this truth, they would never complain. By causing us death He would procure us life; for all our happiness, spiritual, temporal, and eternal, consists in resigning ourselves to God, to do in us and with us as He pleases, and with so much the more submission, as things please us less. By this pure dependence on His Spirit, everything is given us admirably. If the soul were faithful to leave itself in the hand of God, sustaining all His operations, whether gratifying or mortifying, suffering itself to be conducted, from moment to moment, by His hand, and annihilated by the strokes of His Providence, without complaining, or desiring anything but what it has, it would soon arrive at the experience of the eternal truth, though it might not at once know the ways by which God conducted it there.

But people want to direct God, instead of resigning themselves to be directed by Him. To show Him a way, instead of passively following where He leads. Hence, many called to enjoy God Himself, and not barely His gifts, spend all their lives in running after little consolations, and making their happiness to consist therein.

I had an internal strife, which continually racked me; two powers appeared equally strong, seemed equally to struggle for the mastery within me. On the one hand, a desire of pleasing God; on the other, the view of the depravity of my heart, and the continual rising of self. Oh, what torrents of tears, what desolations! "Is it possible," I cried, "that I have received so many graces and favors from God, only to lose them; that I have loved Him with so much ardor, but to be eternally deprived of Him; that His benefits have only produced ingratitude; His fidelity been repaid with infidelity; that my heart has been emptied of all creatures, and created objects, and filled with His blessed presence and love, now to be wholly void of Divine power, and only filled with wanderings and created objects!"

I could now no longer pray as formerly. Heaven seemed shut to me, and I thought justly. I could get no consolation, nor make any complaint; nor had I any creature on earth to whom I might impart my condition. I found myself banished from all beings, without support or refuge in anything. I could no more practice any virtue with facility; such as had formerly been so familiar seemed to have left me. "Alas!" said I, "is it possible this heart, formerly all on fire, should become like ice!" Whatever I tried for a remedy seemed only to increase the malady. Tears were my drink and sorrow my food. I felt such pain as I never could bring any one to comprehend, but such as have experienced it. I had within myself an executioner who tortured me without respite. Even when I went to church, I was not easy there. To sermons I could give no attention: they were of no service or refreshment. I scarcely understood anything in them.

CHAPTER XIII.

As my husband drew near his end, his distempers had no intermission. No sooner was he recovered from one but he fell into another. He bore great pains with much patience, offering them to God, and making a good use of them. Yet his anger toward me increased, because reports were multiplied to him, and those about him did nothing but vex him. The maid, who used to torment me, sometimes took pity on me. She came as soon as I was gone into my closet, and said: "Come to my master, that your mother-in-law may not speak any more to him against you."

My husband having, sometime before his death, finished building the chapel in the country, where we spent part of the summer, I had the conveniency of prayers daily, and the communion. They solemnized the dedication of this little chapel, and though I had already begun to enter into the condition described, when they began to bless it, I felt myself inwardly siezed, which continued more than five hours, all the time of the ceremony, when our Lord made a new consecration of me to Himself. I seemed to myself a temple consecrated to Him, for time and eternity; and said within myself, speaking both of one and the other: "May this temple never be profaned; may the praises of God be sung therein forever!" It seemed as if my prayer was granted. But soon this was taken from me, and not so much as a remembrance left to console me.

At this country house, a little place of retreat before the chapel was built, I retired for prayer to woods and caverns. God preserved me from dangerous and venomous beasts. Sometimes, unawares, I kneeled upon serpents, there in great plenty; and they fled away without doing me harm. Once I was alone in a little wood, where was a mad bull; but, without offering me the least hurt, he betook himself to flight. If I could recount all the providences of God it would appear wonderful. They were so frequent and continual, I could but be astonished at them. God everlastingly gives to such as have nothing to repay Him. If there appears in the creature any fidelity or patience, it is He alone who gives it. If He ceases for an instant to support,—if He seems to leave me to myself, I cease to be strong, and find myself weaker than any other creature. If my miseries show what I am, His favors show what He is, and the extreme necessity of ever depending on Him.

At last, after passing twelve years and four months in the crosses of marriage, as great as possible, except poverty which I never knew, though I had much desired it, God drew me out of that state to give me still stronger crosses to bear, such as I had never met with before. For if you give attention, sir, to the life you have ordered me to write, you will remark that my crosses have been increasing, one being removed to give place to another, still heavier than the former. Amidst the great troubles imposed upon me, when they said I was in a mortal sin, I had nobody in the world to speak to, no support, no confessor, no director, no friend, no counsellor. I had lost all. I remained without any creature; and to complete my distress, I seemed to be left without God Himself, who alone could support me in such deep distress.

My husband's illness grew more obstinate. He apprehended the approach of death, and wished for it, so oppressive was the languishing life he dragged on. To other ills was added so great a dislike to nourishment that he did not take enough to sustain life. I alone had the courage to get him to take what he did. The doctor advised him to go into the country. There for a few days he seemed better, when he was suddenly taken with a complication of diseases. His patience increased with his pain. I saw he could not live long. It was a great trouble to me, that my mother-in-law kept me from him as much as she could, and infused into his mind such a displeasure against me; I was afraid he would die in it. I took a little time when she was not with him, and kneeling said if I had ever done anything that displeased him I begged his pardon, assuring him it had not been voluntary. He was much affected, and as he had just come out of a sound sleep, said to me: "It is I who beg your pardon. I did not deserve you." After that he was not only pleased to see me, but gave me advice what I should do after his death; not to depend on the people on whom I now depended. He was for eight days resigned and patient, though on account of the prevailing gangrene, he was cut and opened with a lance. I sent to Paris for the most skillful surgeon; but when he arrived my husband was dead.

No mortal could die in a more Christian disposition, or with more courage after having received the sacrament in a manner truly edifying. I was not present when he expired, for out of tenderness he made me retire. He was above twenty hours unconscious and in agonies of death. Thou didst order, O my God, that he should die on Magdalene's eve, to show me I was to be wholly Thine. I renewed every year, on Magdalene's day, the marriage-contract which I made to Thee, my Lord; and I found myself at that time free to renew it, and that most solemnly. It was in the morning of July

21st, 1676, that he died. Next day I entered into my closet, and renewed my marriage-contract, and added thereto a vow of chastity. After that I was filled with great interior joy, new to me, as for a long time I had been plunged in the deepest bitterness.

As soon as I heard that my husband had expired, "Oh, my God," I cried, "Thou hast broken my bonds, and I will offer Thee a sacrifice of praise." After that I remained in a deep silence, both exterior and interior, quite dry and without any support. I could neither weep nor speak. My mother-in-law said fine things, and was much commended by everyone. They were offended at my silence, which they attributed to want of resignation.

I was much exhausted; for though I was but recently delivered of my daughter, I attended and sat up with my husband four and twenty nights before his death. I was more than a year recovering the fatigue, joined to my great weakness and pain, both of body and mind. The great depression and stupidity I was in, was such I could not say a word about God. It bore me down in such a manner I could hardly speak.

I saw crosses would not fail, since my mother-in-law had survived my husband. I was still tied, having two children so short a time before my husband's death, the effect of Divine wisdom; for had I only my eldest son, I would have put him in college, and gone into the convent of the Benedictines, and frustrated all the designs of God.

I was willing to show the esteem I had for my husband in causing the most magnificent funeral to be made for him, at my own expense. I paid off the legacies he left. My mother-in-law violently opposed everything I could do for my own interests. I had nobody to apply to for advice or help; my brother would not give me the least assistance. I was ignorant of business affairs; but God supplied me with such a perfect intelligence that I succeeded. I omitted not the least minutia, and was surprised that I should know without ever having learned. I digested all my papers, and regulated all my affairs, without assistance. My husband had abundance of writings deposited in his hands. I took an exact inventory of them, and sent them severally to their owners, which, without Divine assistance, would have been difficult for me; because, my husband having been long sick, everything was in great confusion. This gained me the reputation of being a skillful woman.

There was one matter of great importance. A number of persons, who had been contending at law for years, applied to my husband to settle their affairs. Though it was not properly the business of a gentleman, they applied to him because he had understanding and prudence; and as he had a love for several of them, he consented. There were twenty actions and twenty-two persons concerned, who could not get any end put to their differences, by reason of new incidents continually falling out. My husband got lawyers to examine the papers, but died before he could make any procedure. After his death I sent for them to give them their papers, but they would not receive them, begging that I would accommodate them, and prevent their ruin. It appeared to me as ridiculous, as impossible, to undertake an affair of so great consequence, and which would require so long a discussion. Nevertheless, relying on God, I consented. I shut myself up thirty days in my closet, for all these affairs, without going out but to mass and to meals. The arbitration prepared, they all signed it without seeing it. They were all so well satisfied therewith, they published it everywhere. It was God alone who did those things; for after they were settled I knew nothing about them, and if I hear any talk of such things, it sounds like Arabic.

Being a widow, my crosses increased. That turbulent domestic I have mentioned became more furious than ever. In our house she had amassed a good fortune, and I settled on her, besides, an annuity for life, for services done my husband. She swelled with vanity and haughtiness. Having been used to sit up so much with an invalid, she had taken to drink wine, to keep up her spirits. This had passed into a habit. As she grew aged and weak, a little affected her. I tried to hide this fault; but it could not be concealed. I spoke to her confessor, that he might try, softly and artfully, to reclaim her from it; but instead of profiting by her director's advice, she was outrageous against me. My mother-in-law, who could hardly bear the fault of intemperance, and had often spoken to me about it, now joined in reproaching me and vindicating her. This strange creature, when any company came, would cry out with all her might, that I had dishonored her, and thrown her into despair, and would be the cause of her damnation, as I was taking the ready course to my own. God gave me an unbounded patience. I answered only with mildness all her passionate invectives, giving her every possible mark of affection. If any other maid came to wait on me, she would drive her back in a rage, crying out, that I hated her on account of the affection with which she had served my husband. When she had not a mind to come, I was obliged to serve myself; and when she did come, it was to chide me and make a noise. When I was ill, this girl would be in despair. From hence I thought it was from Thee, O Lord, that all this came upon me; for without Thy permission, she was scarcely capable of such unaccountable conduct. She seemed not sensible of any faults, but always to think herself right. All those whom Thou hast made use of to cause me to suffer, thought they were rendering service to Thee in so doing.

In the place where I lived, I met with one whose doctrine was suspected, but who possessed a dignity in the church, which obliged me to have a deference for him. As he understood how averse I was to all unsound in the faith, and knowing I had some credit in the place, he used his utmost efforts to engage me in his sentiments. I answered him with so much clearness, he had not a word to reply. This increased his desire to contract a friendship for me. He continued to importune me for two years. As he was polite, obliging, and learned, I did not mistrust him, but even conceived a hope of his conversion, in which I found myself mistaken. I then ceased going near him, and broke off all acquaintance with him. Therefore he and his party raised up strong persecutions against me.

These gentlemen had a method by which they knew who were of their party, and who opposite. They sent circular letters, by means of which they cried me down, after a strange manner. This gave me little trouble. I was glad of my new liberty, intending never again to enter into an intimacy with anyone.

The inability I was now in, of doing exterior acts of charity, served this person with a pretext to publish that it was owing to him I had formerly done them; and that, having broken off from him, I now quitted them. He went so far as to preach against me publicly, as one who had been a bright pattern, but was now a scandal. Though I was present at those sermons, and they were enough to weigh me down with confusion, for they offended all that heard them, I could not be troubled, for I thought I merited worse than all he could say, and that, if all men knew me, they would trample me under their feet. My reputation was blasted by this ecclesiastic. Confused like a criminal that dare not lift his eyes, I looked upon the virtue of others with respect. I saw no fault in others, and no virtue in myself. When any happened to praise me, it was like a heavy blow, and I said: "They little know my miseries, and from what state I have fallen." When any blamed me, I agreed to it as right. If I tried to make an outward appearance of righteousness, by the practice of some good thing, my heart in secret rebuked me as guilty of hypocrisy, in wanting to appear what I was not; and God did not permit that to succeed. Oh, how excellent are the crosses of Providence! All other crosses are of no value.

CHAPTER XIV.

The Lord took from me all the sensibility I had for the creatures, even in an instant, as one takes off a robe. Though he had done me that favor, for which I can never be sufficiently grateful, I was neither more contented nor less confused. My God seemed so estranged and displeased with me, that there remained nothing but the grief of having lost His blessed presence. The loss of my reputation every day increasing, became more sensible to my heart, though I was not allowed to justify or bewail myself.

As I became more impotent for every kind of exterior works, as I could not go to see the poor, nor stay at church, nor practice prayer; and as I became colder towards God, in proportion as I was more sensible of my wrong steps, all this destroyed me the more in my own eyes and those of others. Some considerable gentlemen made proposals for me during the depth of my outward and inward desolation. But if a king had presented himself to me, I would have refused him with pleasure, to show Thee, O my God, that with all my miseries I was resolved to be Thine alone; and that if Thou wouldst not accept me, I should at least have the consolation of having been faithful to Thee.

I was for weeks at the last extremity. I could not take any nourishment. A spoonful of broth made me faint. My voice was so gone, that when they put their ears close to my mouth, they could scarcely distinguish my words. I could not see any hope of salvation, yet was not unwilling to die, as I bore a strong impression that the longer I lived the more I would sin. Of the two, I would rather choose hell than sin. All the good, which God made me do, now seemed evil, or full of faults. All my prayers, penances, alms, and charities, seemed to rise up against me and heighten my condemnation. There appeared on the side of God, on my own, and from all creatures, one general condemnation. Then I turned my eyes on every side, to see what way succor might come to me; but my succor could come no way but from Him who made heaven and earth. As I saw there was no safety for me, or spiritual health in myself, I entered into a secret complacency in seeing no good in myself whereon to rest for salvation. The nearer my destruction appeared, the more I found in God Himself wherewith to augment my trust, notwithstanding He seemed so justly irritated against me. It seemed to me that I had in Jesus Christ all that was wanting in myself. Oh, Holy Jesus! I was that lost sheep of the House of Israel whom Thou wast come to save.

The first person God used to draw me to Himself, to whom I had written from time to time, wrote to me in the depth of my distress, desiring me to write to him no more, signifying his disapprobation of what came from me, and that I displeased God greatly. A father, a Jesuit, who had esteemed me much, wrote to me in like manner. I thanked them for their charity, and commended myself to their prayers. It was so indifferent to me to be decried, even of the greatest saints, it added little to my pain. The pain of displeasing God, and the strong propensity I felt to all sorts of faults, caused me most sensible pain.

I was obliged to go on business to a town where a near relation of my mother-in-law lived. When I was there before, she entertained me in a most elegant and obliging manner, regaling me from house to house with emulation. Now she treated me with the utmost contempt, saying she did it to revenge what I made their relation suffer. As I saw that, notwithstanding all my care to please her, I did not succeed, I resolved to come to an explanation with her. I told her there was a current report that I treated her ill, though I made it my study to give her every mark of my esteem. If the report were true, I desired her to allow me to remove, for that I would not choose to stay to give her pain. She answered coldly, I might do what I would, for she had not spoken about it, but was resolved to live apart from me. This was fairly giving me my discharge, and I thought of taking measures privately to retire.

I was in a great strait; on one side fearing lest I was shunning the cross, on the other thinking it unreasonable to impose my stay on one to whom it was painful. Her behavior still continued. When I went into the country to take a little repose, she complained that I left her alone. When I returned to town she could not bear to speak to me or see me. I accosted her without appearing to notice how she received it; but instead of making me any answer, she turned away. I often sent her my coach, desiring her to come and spend a day in the country. She sent it back empty, without any answer. If I passed some days there without sending it, she complained aloud. All I did to please her soured her, God so permitting it; for she had a good heart, but an uneasy temper. I do not fail to think myself under much obligation to her. On Christmas day, I said with much affection: "My mother, on this day was the King of Peace born, to bring it to us; I beg peace of you in His name." I think that touched her.

CHAPTER XV.

An obscure path is the surest to mortify the soul, as it leaves it not any prop to lean upon. The impure, selfish soul is hereby purified, as gold in the furnace. Full of its own judgment, and its own will before; it now obeys like a child, and finds no other will in itself. Before, it would have contested for a trifle; now, it yields at once, not with reluctance and pain, but naturally. Its own vices are vanished. This creature so vain before, now loves poverty, littleness and humiliation. Before, it preferred itself, above everybody; now, everybody above itself, having a boundless love for its neighbor, to bear with his faults. The wolf is changed to the lamb.

During all the time of my deep trials, I went after no fine sights or recreations. When others went, I stayed home. I wanted to know nothing but Jesus Christ. My closet was my only diversion. Even when the queen was near me, whom I had never seen, and whom I had desire to see, I had only to open my eyes, and look out to see her, yet did not do it. I had been fond of hearing others sing; yet I was once four days with one who passed for the finest voice in the world, without ever desiring her to sing; which surprised her, because she was not ignorant that I knew the charming excellence of her voice. However, I committed some infidelities, in inquiring what others said of me by way of blame. I met with one who told me everything. And though I showed nothing of it, it served only to mortify me, as I saw that self-love and nature had put me upon this inquiry.

One of the things which gave me most pain in the seven years, especially the last five, was so strange a folly of my imagination that it gave me no rest. My senses bore it company in such sort that I could no more shut my eyes at church. Thus, having all the gates open, I was like a vineyard exposed, because the hedges the Father had planted were torn away. I saw every one that came and went, and everything that passed in the church. For the same force, which had drawn me inward to recollection, seemed to push me outward to dissipation.

Laden with miseries, weighed down with oppressions, and crushed under continued crosses, there remained in me not the least hope of ever emerging out of distress. But I longed to do what I could for God, though I feared I should never love Him; and seeing the happy state from whence I had fallen, I wished in gratitude to serve Him, though I looked on myself as a victim doomed to destruction. Sometimes the view of that happy period caused secret desires to spring up in my heart, of recovering it again; but I was instantly thrown back into the abyss, from whence I could scarcely utter a sigh; I judged myself to be in a state due to unfaithful souls. I seemed, O my God, as if forever cast off from Thy regard, and from that of all creatures. By degrees my state ceased to be painful. I became insensible to it, and my insensibility seemed like the final hardening of my reprobation. My coldness appeared a mortal coldness. And it was, O my God, since I thus died to self, in order to live wholly in Thee, and in Thy precious love. A servant of mine wanted to become a Barnabite. I wrote about it to Father de la Mothe; he answered me, that I must address Father La Combe, the superior of the Barnabites of Tonon. That obliged me to write to him.

I was glad of this opportunity of recommending myself to his prayers. I wrote that I was miserable, and a subject of compassion; and that, far from having advanced towards God, I was entirely alienated from Him. He answered me by a supernatural light, notwithstanding the frightful description I had given of myself, that my condition was of grace. But I could not believe it.

Geneva came into my mind, in a singular manner, which caused me many fears. "What," said I, "to complete my reprobation shall I go to such an excess of impiety, as to quit the faith through apostacy? (The inhabitants of Geneva being generally Protestant Calvinists.) Am I then about quitting that church, for which I would give a thousand lives?" A letter, from Father La Combe, in which he wrote an account of his present disposition, somewhat similiar to mine, restored peace to my mind. I felt myself inwardly united to him, as to a person of great fidelity to the grace of God. Afterwards a woman appeared to me in a dream from heaven, to tell me God demanded me at Geneva.

About ten days before Magdalene's day, 1680, I wrote to Father La Combe, to request him, if he received my letter before that day, to pray particularly for me. Contrary to my expectations, he received my letter on St. Magdalene's eve, and when praying for me the next day, it was said to him, thrice over, with much power: "Ye shall both dwell in the same place." He was surprised, as he never had received interior words before.

On that happy Magdalene's day, July 22nd, 1680, my soul was perfectly delivered. It had already begun, since the receipt of the first letter from Father La Combe, to recover a new life, like that of a dead person raised, though not yet unbound from his grave-clothes. But on this day I was in perfect life, and set wholly at liberty.

I found myself as much raised above nature, as before I had been depressed. I was inexpressibly overjoyed to find Him, whom I thought I had lost forever, returned to me with unspeakable magnificence and purity. Then, O my God, I found again in Thee with new advantages, in an ineffable manner, all I had been deprived of; and the peace I now possessed was all holy, heavenly and inexpressible; all that I enjoyed before was only a peace, a gift of God: now I possessed the God of peace.

I hoped I should enjoy this happy state for some time, but little did I think my happiness so great and immutable as it was. If one may judge of a good by the trouble which precedes it, I leave mine to be judged of by the sorrows I had undergone before attaining it. One day of this happiness was worth more than years of suffering.

An alacrity for doing good was restored to me, greater than ever. At the beginning, this liberty was less extensive; but as I advanced it grew still greater. I had occasion to see M. Bertot, and told him, I thought my state much changed. He, attentive to something else, answered: "No." I believed him, for grace taught me to prefer the judgment of others, rather than my own. This did not give me any trouble; for every state seemed equally indifferent if I only had the favor of God. I felt a kind of beatitude every day increasing in me. I did all sorts of good, without selfishness or premeditation. Whenever a self-reflective thought was presented to my mind, it was instantly rejected. My imagination was kept so fixed, I had little trouble on that head. I wondered at the clearness of my mind and purity of my heart.

Father La Combe wrote that God had great designs in regard to me. "Let them be," said I, "either of justice or mercy, all is equal to me." I still had Geneva deeply at heart, but said nothing, waiting for God to make known to me His all powerful will, satisfied, if He should require anything of me, He would furnish me with the means of performing it. I held myself in readiness to execute His orders, whenever He should make them known, though it were to the laying down of my life. I was released from all crosses. I resumed my care of the sick, and dressing of wounds, and God gave me power to cure the most desperate. When surgeons could do no more, or were going to cut off limbs, then God made me cure them.

Oh, the joy that accompanied me everywhere, finding still Him who had united me to Himself, in His own immensity. How truly did I experience what He said by the four Evangelists, and by one of them twice over: "Whosoever will lose his life for my sake shall find it; and whosoever will save his life shall lose it."

When I had lost all created supports, and even Divine ones, I then found myself happily compelled to fall into the pure Divine, through those very things which seemed to remove me further from it. In losing all gifts, all supports, I found the Giver. In losing the sense and perception of Thee in myself—I found Thee, O my God, to lose Thee no more in Thyself, in Thy own immutability. Oh, poor creatures, who pass all your time in feeding upon the gifts of God, and think therein to be the most favored, how I pity you if you stop here, short of the true rest, and cease to go forward to God Himself, through the loss of those cherished gifts you now delight in. How many pass all their lives in this way, and think highly of themselves therein! Others called of God to die to themselves, pass all their time in a dying life, and inward agonies, without ever entering into God, through death and total loss of self, because they are always willing to retain something, and so never lose themselves to the whole extent of the designs of God. Wherefore, they never enjoy God in all His fulness; a loss that can not be perfectly known in this life.

Oh, my Lord, what happiness did I not largely taste in my solitude, and with my little family, where nothing interrupted my tranquility! Thou, O my God, dealt by me as by Thy servant Job, rendering me double for all Thou hadst taken from me, and delivering me from all my crosses. Thou gavest me a marvelous facility to satisfy everyone. My mother-in-law declared that none could be better satisfied with me than she was. Such as before had cried me down the most, now testified their sorrow for it, and became full of my praises. My reputation was established. I remained in an entire peace, without as within. My soul seemed like that New Jerusalem, prepared as a bride for her husband, and where there is no more sorrow, or sighing. I had a perfect indifference to everything, and an union so great with the good will of God, my own will seemed entirely lost.

These dispositions have grown stronger, and more perfect even to this hour. I could neither desire one thing nor another, but was content with whatever fell out, without any reflection thereon, or any attention thereto, except when any asked me: "Will you have this, or that?" And then I was surprised to find there was nothing in me, which could desire or choose. It seemed to me, as if my soul was wholly passed into its God, to make but one and the same thing with Him; even as a little drop of water, cast into the sea, receives the qualities of the sea. Oh, union of unity, demanded of God by Jesus Christ for men, and merited by Him! How strong is this in a soul that is become lost in its God!

CHAPTER XVI.

I was obliged to go to Paris on business. Having entered a church, that was dark, I went up to the first confessor, whom I did not know, nor have ever seen since. I made a simple, short prayer of confession; but to the confessor I said not a word. He surprised me in saying: "I know not who you are, whether maid, wife or widow; but I exhort you to do what the Lord has made known to you, that He requires of you." I answered him: "Father, I am a widow who has little children. What else would God require of me, but to take care of them in their education?" He replied: "I know not. You know if God requires something of you; nothing in this world ought to hinder you from doing His will. One may have to leave one's children to do that." This surprised me. I told him nothing of Geneva. I disposed myself submissively to quit everything, if the Lord required it of me.

I lived with my family in great tranquility, until one of my friends had a great desire to go on a mission to Siam. He lived twenty leagues from my house. As he was ready to make a vow to this purpose, he found himself stopped, with an impulse to come and speak to me. He came, and told me his intention. I felt an impression to relate to him my case, and the idea I had for Geneva. I told him a dream I had, and said to him: "You must go to Siam; and also serve me in this affair. For that end God has sent you hither; I desire your advice." After three days, having consulted the Lord, he told me he believed I was to go thither; but to be the better assured to see the Bishop of Geneva; if he approved of my design, it would be a sign that it was from the Lord; if not, I must drop it. I fell in with his sentiment. He offered to go to Annecy, to speak to the Bishop, and to bring me a faithful account of what they should agree on. As he was advanced in years, we were deliberating in what way he could take so long a journey, when there came two travelers, who told us the Bishop was at Paris. This was an extraordinary providence. He spoke to the Bishop at Paris, and I, having occasion to go thither, spoke to him also.

I told him my design was to go into the country, to employ there my substance, to erect an establishment for all such as should be willing to give themselves to God without reserve. The Bishop approved the design. He said: "There are New Catholics going to establish themselves at Gex, near Geneva, and it is providential." I answered: "I have no vocation for Gex, but for Geneva." He said I might go from hence to that city. I went to see the prioress of the New Catholics at Paris. She seemed much rejoiced, and assured me she would join me. As she is a great servant of God, this confirmed me. I thought God would make choice of her for her virtue, and me for my worldly substance; for when I inadvertently looked at myself, I could not think God would make use of me; but when I saw the things in God, then I perceived that the more I was nothing, the fitter I was for His designs. I saw nothing in myself extraordinary, and imagined that an extraordinary degree of inspiration was necessary for extraordinary designs. This made me hesitate and fear deception. I did not yet sufficiently comprehend that to follow, step by step, the guidance of Divine Providence was the greatest and purest light. Not that I was in fear of anything, as to my perfection which I had referred to God; but I was afraid of not doing His will by being too ardent and hasty. I went to consult Father Claude Martin. He gave me no decisive answer, demanding time to pray about it, saying he would write what should appear to him to be the will of God. M. Bertot told me my design was of God; he had had a sense given him of God, that He required something of me. I returned home to set everything in order. I loved my children much, having great satisfaction in being with them, but resigned all to God to follow His will.

On my return from Paris, I left myself in the hands of God, resolved not to take any step, either to make the thing succeed or hinder it, but singly to move as He should be pleased to direct me. I had mysterious dreams, which portended crosses, persecutions and afflictions.

I saw near me a little animal which appeared dead. This animal I took to be the envy of some persons, which seemed to have been dead for some time. I took it up, and as it strove to bite me, and magnified to the eye, I cast it away; but found it filled my fingers with sharp-pointed prickles like needles. I came to an acquaintance to get him to take them out, but he pushed them deeper in, and left me so till a charitable priest, of great merit (whose countenance is still present with me, though I have not yet seen him, but believe I shall before I die), took this animal up with a pair of pincers. As soon as he held it fast, those sharp prickles fell off. Then I found I easily entered a place, before inaccessible. And though the mire was up to my girdle, in my way to a deserted church, I went over it, without getting any dirt. It will be easy to see in the sequel what this signified.

You will wonder that I relate dreams. I do this out of fidelity, having promised to omit nothing of what should come into my mind; because it is the method God makes use of to communicate Himself to faithful souls, to give them foretokens of things to come. Mysterious dreams are found in the Scriptures. They have singular properties, as—

1. To leave a certainty that they are mysterious, and will have their effect in their season;

2. To be hardly ever effaced out of the memory, though one forgets all others;

3. To redouble the certainty of their truth every time one thinks of them;

4. They generally leave a certain unction, a divine savor at one's waking.

I received letters from sundry religious persons, some of whom lived far from me, and from one another, relating to my going forth in the service of God, and some of them mentioned Geneva. One intimated I must there bear the cross and be persecuted; and another that I should be eyes to the blind, feet to the lame, and arms to the maimed.

The ecclesiastic of our house was afraid I was under a delusion; but Father Claude Martin wrote that, after many prayers, the Lord had given him to know that He required me at Geneva, and to make a free sacrifice of everything to Him. I answered that perhaps the Lord required of me nothing more than a sum of money to assist in founding an institution to be established there. He replied, that the Lord had made him know that He wanted not my worldly substance but myself. At the same time Father La Combe wrote that the Lord had given him a certainty that He wanted me at Geneva. The writers of these two letters lived above a hundred and fifty leagues from each other; yet both wrote the same thing.

As soon as I became fully convinced of its being the will of the Lord, my senses had some pain about leaving my children. A doubt seized my mind. O my Lord! Had I rested on myself, or on the creatures, I would have revolted, and leaned on a broken reed. But relying on Thee alone, I resolved to go, regardless of the censures of such as understood not what it is to be a servant of the Lord and obey His orders. I firmly believed that He, by His Providence, would furnish the means necessary for the education of my children.

Whilst Providence appointed my forsaking all things, it seemed to make my chains stronger, and my separation the more blameable; for none could receive stronger marks of affection from an own mother than those I received from my mother-in-law; even the least sickness which befell me made her uneasy. She said she had veneration for my virtue. I believe what contributed not a little to this change was, that three persons had offered suit to me, and I had refused them, though their fortune and quality were superior to mine. She remembered how she had upbraided me on this head, and I answered her not a word. She began to fear lest such rigorous treatment might excite me to deliver myself by such means, with honor, from her tyranny, and was sensible what damage that might be to my children. She was now tender to me on every occasion.

I fell extremely ill. My mother-in-law went not from my bedside; her many tears proved the sincerity of her affection. I was much affected at it, and loved her as my true mother. How, then, should I leave her now, being so far advanced in age? The maid, who till then had been my plague, took an inconceivable friendship for me, praised me everywhere, and served me with extraordinary respect. She begged pardon for all she had made me suffer, and died of grief after my departure.

There was a nun in a monastery I often went to, who was entered into a state of purification, which everyone in the house looked on as distraction. They locked her up, which like to have destroyed her. All that went to see her called it frenzy or melancholy. I knew her to be devout. I requested to see her. I felt an impression that she sought purity. I desired of the Superior that she should not be locked up, nor people be admitted to see her, but that she would confide her to my care. I discovered her greatest pain was at being counted a fool. I advised her to bear the state of foolishness, since Jesus Christ had been willing to bear it before Herod. This sacrifice gave her a calmness at once. But as God was willing to purify her soul, He separated her from all those things for which she had the greatest attachment. At last, after she had patiently undergone her sufferings, her Superior wrote to me that I was right, and she had now come out of that state of dejection, in greater purity than ever. This was the commencement of the gift of discerning spirits.

The winter before I left home was one of the longest and hardest that had been for several years, viz., 1680. It was followed with extreme scarcity, which proved an occasion of exercising charity. My mother-in-law joined me. We distributed at the house ninety-six dozen loaves of bread every week, but the private charities to the bashful poor were much greater. I kept poor boys and girls employed at work. And the Lord gave such blessings to my alms, I did not find that my family lost by it. Before the death of my husband, my mother-in-law told him that I would ruin him with my charities, and he commanded me to set down in writing all the money I laid out for the expense of the house, and all that I caused to be bought, that from thence he might judge of what I gave to the poor. This appeared so much the harder, as for above eleven years we had been married I never before had this required of me. What troubled me most was the fear of having nothing to give to such as wanted. I submitted to it, without retrenching my charities. I did not set down any of my alms, yet my account of expenses was found to answer exactly. I was much surprised and astonished, and esteemed it one of the wonders of Providence.

How much is there in the world of useless dissipation, which, properly applied, might amply serve for the subsistence of the poor, and would abundantly be restored, and amply rewarded to the families of those who gave it?

In my greatest trials, some years after my husband's death (for they began three years before my widowhood, and lasted four years after), my footman came one day to tell me, for I was then in the country, that there was in the road a poor soldier dying. I had him brought in, and kept him above a fortnight. His malady was a flux. It was so nauseous, that though the domestics were charitably inclined, nobody could bear him. I went myself to take away his vessels. I never did anything of the kind so hard to me. When I emptied them, there was such an intolerable stench, I was ready to faint. I frequently made efforts for a full quarter of an hour. It seemed as if my very heart was going to come up; yet I never desisted from doing it. I sometimes kept poor people at my house to dress their most putrid sores, but never met with anything so terrible as this. The poor man, after I made him receive the sacrament, died.

What gave me no small concern was the tenderness I had for my children, especially my younger son, whom I had strong reasons for loving. I saw him inclined to be good, and everything seemed to favor the hopes I had of him. I thought it running a great risk to leave him to another's education. My daughter I designed to take with me, though she was ill of a tedious fever. She speedily recovered. The ties, with which the Lord held me closely united to Himself, were infinitely stronger than those of flesh and blood. The laws of my sacred marriage obliged me to give up all, to follow my Spouse whithersoever it was His pleasure to call me. Though I often hesitated, and doubted much before I went, I never doubted after my going, of its being His will. The gospel has promised to those that leave all for the love of the Lord, "an hundred fold in this life, and persecutions also." And have not I infinitely more than an hundred fold, in so entire a possession as Thou, my Lord, hast taken of me; in that unshaken firmness which Thou givest me in my sufferings; in a perfect tranquility in the midst of a furious tempest, which assaults me on every side; in an unspeakable joy, enlargedness and liberty, in a straight and rigorous captivity. I have no desire that my imprisonment should end before the right time. I love my chains. Everything is equal to me, as I have no will of my own, but purely the love and will of Him who possesses me.

I was not so reluctant to go with the New Catholics, as to engage with them, not finding a sufficient attraction, though I sought for it. I longed indeed to contribute to the conversion of souls, and God made use of me to convert several families before my departure, one composed of eleven persons. Besides, Father La Combe had written to me, to make use of this opportunity for setting off, but did not tell me whether I ought to engage with them or not. Thus God alone ordered everything.

One day, before going through infidelity, reflecting humanly on this undertaking of mine, I found my faith staggering, weakened with a fear lest I were under a mistake, which slavish fear was increased by an ecclesiastic at our house, who told me it was a rash design. Being a little discouraged, I opened the Bible to this passage, "Fear not, thou worm Jacob, and ye men of Israel; I will help thee, saith the Lord, and thy Redeemer, the Holy One of Israel" (Isa. xli. 14), and near it, "Fear not: for I have redeemed thee, I have called thee by thy name; thou art mine. When thou passest through the waters, I will be with thee" (Isa. xliii. 1, 2).

I had great courage given me for going, but could not persuade myself it would be best to settle with the New Catholics. It was necessary to see Sister Garnier, their Superior at Paris, in order to take our measures together. But I could not go to Paris, because that journey would have hindered me from taking another, which I had to take. She, though much indisposed, resolved to come and see me.

Sister Garnier did not declare her thoughts to me for four days. Then she told me she would not go with me. I was surprised, as I had persuaded myself that God would grant to her virtue what He might refuse to my demerits. Besides, the reasons she gave appeared human, and void of supernatural grace. That made me hesitate a little; then, taking new courage, through the resignation of my whole self, I said: "As I go not thither for your sake, I will not fail to go even without you." This surprised her, for she thought that, on her refusal, I would decline going.

CHAPTER XVII.

I went to the New Catholics at Paris, where Providence wrought wonders to conceal me. They sent for the notary who had drawn up the contract of engagement. When he read it, I felt such a repugnance, I could not bear to sign it. The notary wondered, and more so, when Sister Garnier came in, and told him there needed no contract of engagement. I was enabled through Divine assistance to put my affairs in good order, and write letters by the inspiration of the Spirit, which I had never experienced before.

I took with me only my daughter and two maids. We set off in a boat on the river, though I had taken places in the stage-coach, that, if they searched for me in the coach, they might not find me. I went to Melun to wait for it there.

In this boat the child could not forbear making crosses, employing a person to cut rushes for her to use. She put around, all over me, above three hundred. I let her do it. It was not without its meaning. I felt an interior certainty that I was going to meet with crosses in abundance. Sister Garnier, who saw that they could not restrain her from covering me with crosses, said, "What that child does appears significant," and turning to the little girl, she said, "Give me some crosses, too, my pretty pet." "No," she replied, "they are all for my dear mother." Soon she gave her one to stop her importunity, then continued putting more on me; after which she desired some river-flowers to be given her; and braiding a garland put it on my head, and said, "After the cross you shall be crowned." I admired all this in silence, and offered myself up to the pure love of God, as a victim, willing to be sacrificed to Him.

Some time before my departure, a friend related to me a vision she had respecting me. She saw my heart surrounded with thorns; our Lord appeared in it well pleased; the thorns seemed likely to tear it, yet instead they only rendered it fairer, and our Lord's approbation the stronger.

At Corbeil (a little town on the Seine, sixteen miles south of Paris), I met with the priest God had first used to draw me to His love. He approved of my design to leave all for the Lord; but thought I should not be well suited with the New Catholics. He told me our leadings were incompatible. He cautioned me not to let them know that I walked in the inward path, or I must expect nothing but persecution. But it is vain to contrive to hide when God sees it is best for us to suffer, and our wills are utterly resigned to Him.

At Paris I gave the New Catholics all the money I had. I reserved not a single penny, rejoicing to be poor after the example of Jesus Christ. I brought from home nine thousand livres. As I had reserved nothing to myself, and lent them six thousand, this returned to my children, but none to me, which gives me no trouble; for poverty, thus procured, constitutes my riches. The rest I gave entirely to the sisters. I did not reserve so much as my linen for my own use, putting it in the common fund. I had neither a locked coffer nor purse. I brought but little linen for fear I should be discovered. My persecutors reported I had brought great sums from home, which I had imprudently expended, and given to the friends of Father La Combe, which is false. I had not a penny. On my arrival at Annecy, a poor man asking alms, I gave him the buttons from my sleeves. At another time I gave a poor man a little plain ring I had worn as a token of my marriage with Jesus Christ.

We joined the flying stage at Melun, where I left Sister Garnier, and went on with the other sisters, with whom I had no acquaintance. These carriages were fatiguing, and I got no sleep through so long a journey; and although my daughter, a tender child, five years of age, got scarcely any, yet we bore so great a fatigue without falling sick. This child had not an hour's uneasiness, though she was only three hours in bed every night. At another time, half this fatigue, or even the want of rest, would have thrown me into a fit of sickness. In the coach, my Divine Lord communed with me, in a manner which the others did not perceive. The cheerfulness I showed, in great danger, encouraged them. I sang hymns of joy at finding myself disengaged from the world. God so protected us, He seemed a pillar of fire by night, and a pillar of cloud by day. We passed over a dangerous spot between Lyons and Chamberry. Our carriage broke as we were coming out. Had it happened a little sooner, we must have perished.

We arrived at Annecy on Magdalene's eve, 1681; and on Magdalene's day the Bishop of Geneva performed divine service for us, at the tomb of St. Francis de Sales. There I renewed my spiritual marriage with my Redeemer, as I did every year on this day.

That day we left Annecy, and the next went to prayers at Geneva, at the house of the French resident. I had much joy at the communion, and God more powerfully united me to Himself. That evening we arrived late at Gex, where we found only bare walls; though the

Bishop of Geneva had assured me that the house was furnished, as undoubtedly he believed it to be. We lodged at the house of the Sisters of Charity, who were so kind as to give us their beds.

I was in great pain of mind for my daughter, who visibly fell away. I had a strong desire to place her with the Ursulines at Tonon. My heart was so affected on her behalf, that I could not forbear weeping in secret. I said: "I will take my daughter to Tonon, and leave her there till I see how we be accommodated here." They opposed it strongly, after a manner which seemed hardhearted, seeing she was worn to a skeleton. I looked upon the child as a victim I had sacrificed. I wrote to Father La Combe, entreating him to come and see me, to consult about it. Several days passed without any answer. I became resigned to the will of God.

Our Lord took pity on the lamentable condition of my daughter, and the Bishop of Geneva wrote to Father La Combe, to come as speedily as possible to console us. As soon as I saw that father, I was surprised to feel an interior grace, which I call Communication; such as I had never had before with any person. An influence of grace came from him to me, through the innermost of the soul; and returned from me to him. Like a tide of grace it caused a flux and reflux, flowing on into the divine and invisible ocean. This is a pure, holy union, which God alone operates, which has increased between us. It is an union exempt from all weakness and self-interest, which causes those who are blessed with it to rejoice in beholding themselves, as well as those beloved, laden with crosses and afflictions; an union which has no need of the presence of the body; an union never experienced, but between souls united to God. I never before felt a union of this sort with anyone, and had never heard of the like. I had no doubt of its being from God; so far from turning the mind from Him, it tended to draw it more deeply into Him. It dissipated all my pains, and established me in the most profound peace.

He told me to take my daughter to Tonon, where he thought she would be well situated. And after I had mentioned my dislike to the New Catholics, he told me it would be best for us to stay there, free from all engagements, until God, by His Providence, should make known to me how He would dispose of me.

I had begun to awake regularly at midnight to pray. At this time I awoke with these words: "It is written of me, I will do Thy will, O my God." This was accompanied with the most pure, penetrating, powerful communication of grace I had ever experienced. From midnight I continued on my knees till four in the morning, in prayer, in a sweet intercourse with God, and the same the night following.

The next day, Father La Combe told me he had a great certainty I was a stone God designed for the foundation of some great building. But what that building was he knew no more than I. After whatever manner it is to be, whether His Divine Majesty will make use of me in this life, for some design known to Him only, or make me one of the stones of the New Jerusalem, such stone can not be polished but by the strokes of the hammer; and our Lord has given to this soul of mine the qualities of the stone—firmness, resignation, insensibility, and power to endure hardness under the operations of His hand.

I carried my little daughter to the Ursulines at Tonon. The child took a great fondness for Father La Combe, saying: "He is a good father, one from

God." Here I found a hermit, they called Anselm, a person of extraordinary sanctity, from Geneva. God had miraculously drawn him from thence, at twelve years of age. He had at nineteen taken the habit of hermit of St. Augustine. He and another lived alone in a little hermitage, where they saw nobody but such as came to their chapel. He had lived twelve years in this hut, never eating anything but pulse with salt, and sometimes oil. Three times a week he lived on bread and water. He never drank wine, and generally made but one meal in twenty-four hours. He wore for a shirt a coarse hair cloth, and lodged on the bare ground. He lived in a continual state of prayer, and in the greatest humility. God had done by him many signal miracles.

This good hermit had a great sense of the designs of God on Father La Combe and me. God showed him that strange crosses were preparing for us both, and we were both destined for the aid of souls.

I did not find any suitable place for my daughter at Tonon. I thought myself like Abraham, when going to sacrifice his son. Father La Combe, accosting me said: "Welcome, daughter of Abraham!" To leave her there where scarce anyone understood French, and the food. which she could not take, being so far different from ours, was a great hardship. All my tenderness for her was awakened, and I looked on myself as her destroyer. I experienced what Hagar suffered when she put away her son Ishmael in the desert, that she might not be forced to see him perish. Everything looked dark. God so ordered it, to purify me from too human an attachment. For after I returned from the Ursulines at Tonon, they changed her diet, and gave her what was suitable to her delicacy; whereby she recovered finely.

CHAPTER XVIII.

When it was known in France that I was gone, there was a general outcry. Those who attacked me with the most violence were the human spiritualists. Father de la Mothe wrote me that all persons of learning and of piety united in censuring me. Sister Garnier changed and declared against me.

Here I ate and slept little. The food was putrid and full of worms, by reason of the great heat, and being kept too long; what I formerly beheld with great abhorrence, now became my only nourishment; yet everything was rendered easy. In God I found everything which I had lost for Him. That spirit, which I once thought I had lost in a strange stupidity, was restored to me with inconceivable advantages. I was astonished at myself. There was nothing which I was not fit for, or in which I did not succeed. Those who observed this said I had a prodigious capacity. I knew I had but meagre capabilities, but that in God my spirit had received a quality it never had before. I experienced something of the state the apostles were in, after they received the Holy Spirit. I had every good thing, and no want of anything.

Sometime after my arrival at Gex, the Bishop of Geneva came to see us. He was so clearly convinced, and so much affected, that he could not forbear expressing it. He opened his heart to me. He confessed his own deviations and infidelities. When I spoke he entered into what I said, and acknowledged it to be the truth; as indeed it was the Spirit of truth which inspired me, without which I should be a mere simpleton. He said he had it in mind to give me Father La Combe for director, for he was a man illuminated with God, who understood the inward path, and had a singular gift of pacifying souls. Greatly was I rejoiced when the Bishop appointed him, seeing his authority united with the grace which had given him to me, by a union of supernatural life and love. The fatigues and watchings with my daughter threw me into a violent sickness, attended with exquisite pain. The physicians judged me in danger, and yet the sisters of the house neglected me. The stewardess was so penurious, she did not give me what was necessary to sustain life. I had not a penny, as I had reserved nothing. And they received all the money remitted to me from France, which was considerable. Thus I was in necessity even among those to whom I had given all. They wrote Father La Combe, desiring him to come, as I was extremely ill. He was so touched with compassion, as to walk on foot all night, eight great leagues; but he travelled not otherwise, endeavoring in that, as in everything, to imitate Christ.

As soon as he entered the house, my pains abated; and when he had prayed, laying his hand on my head, I was perfectly cured, to the great astonishment of my physicians, who were not willing to acknowledge the miracle; being not pleased, as they knew we were come on a religious motive, and their sentiments were so opposite to ours. These sisters advised me to return to my daughter. Father La Combe returned with me. A violent storm arose on the lake, which made me sick, and seemed likely to overset the boat. But Providence appeared in our favor; it was taken notice of by the mariners and passengers, who looked upon Father La Combe as a saint. Thus we arrived at Tonon, where I went into a retreat twelve days. Here I made vows of perpetual chastity, poverty and obedience, covenanting to obey whatever I should believe to be the will of God. I found I had perfect chastity of love to the Lord, it being without any reserve, division, or view of interest; perfect poverty, by the total privation of everything that was mine, both inwardly and outwardly; perfect obedience to the will of the Lord, and honor to Jesus Christ in loving Himself only; the effect of which soon appeared. When by the loss of ourselves we pass into the Lord, our will is made one and the same with that of the Lord, according to the prayer of Christ (John xvii. 21). Then the will is rendered marvelous, because it is made the will of the Lord, which is the greatest of miracles; and because it works wonders in Him. For as it is the Lord who wills in the soul, that will has its effect. Scarcely has it willed but the thing is done.

Why then so many oppressions endured? Why do not these souls, if they have such a power, set themselves free? If they had any will to do anything of that sort, against Divine Providence, that would be the will of the flesh, or of man, and not the will of God (John i. 13).

I rose generally at midnight, waking at the proper time; but if I wound up my alarm-watch, then I used not to awake in time. I saw that the Lord had the care of a Father over me. When I had any indisposition, and my body wanted rest, he did not awake me; but I felt in my sleep a singular possession of Him.

The Lord made known to many that He designed me for a mother of great people, simple and child-like. They took these intelligences in a literal sense, and thought it related to some institution. But it appeared to me that the persons whom it would please the Lord that I should win over to Him, and to whom I should be as a mother, should have the same affection for me as children have for a parent, but deeper and stronger; and giving me all that was necessary for them, to bring them to walk in the way by which He would lead them.

I would suppress what I am now about to write if it were my own, because few souls are capable of understanding Divine leadings. I have never read anything like it.

After I had come out of the trying condition, I found it had purified my soul, instead of blackening it, as I feared. I possessed God after a manner pure and immense. In regard to thoughts or desires, all was so clean, so naked, so lost in the divinity, that the soul had no selfish movement, the powers of the mind and the senses being wonderfully purified. Sometimes I was surprised to find there appeared not one selfish thought. The imagination, formerly so restless, now no more troubled me. I had no more perplexity or uneasy reflections. The will, perfectly dead to all its own appetites, void of every human inclination, both natural and spiritual, only inclined to what God pleased. This vast largeness, not bounded by anything, increases every day.

My prayer was in an openness and singleness inconceivable. I was, as it were, borne up on high, out of myself. This ascension of the spirit is not operated till the death of self, wherein the soul comes out of itself to pass into its Divine object. The spirit has so powerful a tendency to its Divine Origin, that if it were not stopped by a continual miracle, its moving quality would cause the body to be drawn after it whithersoever it would, by reason of its impetuosity and noble ascent. But God has given it a terrestrial body for a counterpoise. This spirit then, created to be united to its Origin, without any medium or interstice, feeling itself drawn by its divine object, tends to it with an extreme violence; in such sort that God, suspending for sometime the power which the body has to hold back the spirit, it follows with ardency; but when it is not sufficiently purified to pass into God, it gradually returns back to itself; and as the body resumes its own quality, it turns to the earth. The saints who have been the most perfect have advanced to that degree, as to have nothing of all this, and some have lost it toward the end of their lives. The soul, by death to itself, passes into its Divine Object. The farther I went, the more my spirit was lost in its Sovereign, who attracted it more and more to Himself. He was pleased at first that I should know this for the sake of others, and not for myself. Indeed He drew my soul more and more into Himself, till it lost itself entirely. It seemed to pass into Him. As one sees a river pass into the ocean, lose itself in it, its water for a time distinguished from that of the sea, till it gradually becomes transformed into the same sea, and possesses all its qualities; so was my soul lost in God, who communicated to it His qualities, having drawn it out of all that it had of its own.

To such, the words of our Lord seem addressed: "Your joy no man taketh from you" (John xvi. 22). It is as it were plunged in a river of peace. Its prayer is continual. Nothing can hinder it from praying to God, or loving Him. It amply verifies these words: "I sleep, but my heart waketh" (S. of S. v. 2). Even sleep itself does not hinder it from praying. Oh, unutterable happiness!

Then the soul knows that all the states of self-pleasing visions, openings, ecstasies and raptures, are rather obstacles that do not serve this state which is far above them; because the state which has supports, has pain to lose them. In this are verified the words of an experienced saint: "When I would possess nothing through self-love, everything was given me without going after it." Oh, happy dying of the grain of wheat, which makes it produce an hundred-fold! The soul is then equally disposed to receive from the hand of God either good or evil. It receives both without any selfish emotions, letting them flow and be lost as they come.

After I finished my retreat with the Ursulines at Tonon, I returned through Geneva; and, having found no other means of conveyance, the French resident lent me a horse. I knew not how to ride on horseback, but as he assured me it was a quiet horse, I ventured to mount him. A smith, looking at me with a wild, haggard look, struck the horse a blow just as I got on him, which made him leap. He threw me on the ground with such force they thought I was killed. I fell on my temple. My cheek-bone and two of my teeth were broken. I was supported by an invisible Hand; and in a little time I mounted another horse and had a man by my side to keep me up.

My relations left me in peace at Gex, testifying their esteem for me. They had heard at Paris of my miraculous cure; it made a great noise there. Many persons in reputation for sanctity wrote me. One young lady sent me a hundred pistoles for our house, and told me when we wanted money, I had only to write to her, and she would send me all I could desire. They talked in Paris of printing an account of my sacrifice and the miracle of my recovery. I don't know what prevented it, but this journey, which drew upon me so much applause, served for a pretext for the strange condemnation since passed upon me.

CHAPTER XIX.

My relations did not signify any eager desire for my return. The first thing they proposed a month after my arrival at Gex, was to give up my guardianship, make over all my estate to my children, and reserve an annuity to myself. This proposition to some might have appeared unpleasing; but it was not to me. I had no friend whom I could consult about executing the thing I was free to do. I had now the means of accomplishing the desire I had of being conformable to Jesus Christ, poor, naked, and stripped of all. They sent me an article to execute, and I signed it, not perceiving some clauses. It expressed that, when my children should die, I should inherit nothing of my own estate, but it should devolve to my kindred. There were many other things equally to my disadvantage. Though what I had reserved to myself was sufficient to support me in this place, it was scarcely enough to do so in other places. I gave up my estate with more joy, for being thereby conformed to Jesus Christ, than they could have who asked it from me. It is what I have never repented of, nor had any uneasiness about. What pleasure to lose all for the Lord! The love of poverty, thus contracted, is the kingdom of tranquility.

After the accident of the fall from the horse, from which I wonderfully recovered, the devil began to declare himself more openly mine enemy, to become outrageous. One night something monstrous and frightful presented itself, a kind of face, seen by a glimmering bluish light. I don't know whether the flame itself composed that horrible face, for it was so mixed and passed so rapidly, I could not discern it. My soul rested in its calm assurance, and it appeared no more after that manner. As I arose at midnight to pray, I heard frightful noises in my chamber, and after I lay down they were worse; my bed often shook for a quarter of an hour, and the paper sashes were all burst. Every morning they were found shattered, yet I felt no fear. I arose and lighted my wax-candle to look all over the chamber, and at the sashes, at the time the noise was strongest. As he saw I was afraid of nothing, he left off all on a sudden, and attacked me no more in person, but he stirred up men against me, and that succeeded far better, as they counted it a good thing to do me the worst of injuries.

One of the sisters I brought with me, a beautiful girl, contracted an intimacy with an ecclesiastic, who inspired her with an aversion for me, being well assured that I should advise her not to suffer his visits so frequently. She was undertaking a religious retreat. That ecclesiastic was desirous to induce her to make it as a cloak to his frequent visits. The Bishop of Geneva had given Father La Combe for director to our house, and as he was going to cause retreats to be made, I desired her to wait for him. She submitted against her inclination. I began to talk to her on the subject of inward prayer, and drew her into the practice of it. Our Lord gave such a blessing thereto, that this girl gave herself to Him with her whole heart, and the retreat completely won her over. She then became more reserved toward this ecclesiastic, which enraged him against Father La Combe and me. This proved the source of the persecutions which afterwards befell me. The noise in my chamber ended as these commenced.

This ecclesiastic began to talk privately of me with

much contempt. I took no notice of it. A certain friar came to see him, who mortally hated Father La Combe on account of his regularity. These combined together to force me to quit the house, that they might become masters of it themselves.

I saw crosses in abundance. These words came to my mind: "Who for the joy that was set before him endured the cross" (Heb. xii. 2). I prostrated myself a long time with my face on the ground, earnestly desiring to receive all Thy strokes. Oh, Thou who spared not Thine own Son! Thou couldst find none but Him worthy of Thee, and Thou still findest in Him hearts proper for Thee.

After my arrival at Gex, I saw in a sacred dream Father La Combe fastened to an enormous cross, stripped as they paint our Saviour. I saw around it a frightful crowd, which covered me with confusion, and threw back on me the ignominy of his punishment. He seemed to have more pain, but I more reproaches. I have beheld this fully accomplished.

The ecclesiastic won over to his party one of our sisters, the house-steward, and the prioress. I was of a delicate frame; the good inclination I had did not give strength to my body. I brought two maids with me to serve me; yet, as the community had need of them, I gave them up, not thinking but they would allow them to serve me sometimes, in things I was not able to do myself; for I let them receive all my income, they having had already my first half of this year's annuity. Yet they would not permit either of my maid-servants to do anything for me. By my office of sacristan I was obliged to sweep the church, which was large, and they would not let anyone help me in it. I several times fainted over the broom, and was forced to rest in little corners, quite spent. This obliged me to beg them that they would suffer it sometimes to be swept by some of the strong country girls, New Catholics. At last they consented. I never had washed, and was now obliged to wash all the vestry linen. I took one of my maids, because in attempting it by myself, I had done up the linen most awkwardly. But these sisters pulled her by the arms out of my chamber, telling her she should do her own business. I let it quietly pass, without any objection.

The ecclesiastic went to the Bishop of Geneva, who till then had manifested much esteem for me, and persuaded him it would be proper to secure me to that house, to oblige me to give up to it the annual income I had reserved to myself, and to engage me thereto by making me prioress. He drew the Bishop to enter heartily into this proposition, and to bring it about whatever it should cost him.

The ecclesiastic, having so far carried his point, no longer kept any measures in regard to me. He caused all the letters I sent, and those directed to me, to be stopped; to have it in his power to make what impression he pleased on the minds of others, and that I should neither be able to know it, nor to defend myself, nor send to my friends any account of the manner in which I was treated. As Father La Combe was soon to come, I thought he would soften the violent spirit of this man, and give me advice.

They proposed to me the engagement and post of prioress. I answered the engagement was impossible, since my vocation was elsewhere. And I could not regularly be the prioress, till after passing through the noviciate, in which they all served two years before being engaged; that when I should have done as much,

I should see how God would inspire me. The prioress replied pretty tartly, that if I would ever leave them it were best for me to do it immediately. Yet I did not offer to retire, but continued to act as usual. However, I saw the sky thickening, and storms gathering. The prioress then affected a milder air. She assured me she had a desire, as well as I, to go to Geneva; that I should not engage, but only promise to take her with me, if I went thither. She professed a high esteem for me. I let her know that I had no attraction for the life of the New Catholics, by reason of their intrigues. Several things did not please me. I wanted them to be upright in everything. She said the ecclesiastic told her the intrigues were necessary to give the house a credit in distant parts, and to draw charities from Paris. I answered that if we walked uprightly God would never fail us. He would sooner do miracles for us. I remarked, when men had recourse to artifice, charity grew cold, and kept herself shut up. God alone inspires charity; how, then, is it to be drawn by disguises?

Father La Combe came about the retreats the last time he came to Gex. The prioress asked him whether she would one day be united to me at Geneva. He said: "Our Lord has made known to me that you shall never be established at Geneva." Soon after she died. When he had uttered this declaration, she was enraged against us both. She went directly to that ecclesiastic, who was with the house-steward; and they took measures together to oblige me to engage or retire.

With a design to lay snares for him, the ecclesiastic requested Father La Combe to preach on this text: "The king's daughter is all glorious within" (Psa. xlv. 13). That ecclesiastic, present with his confidant, said it was preached against him, and was full of errors. He drew up eight propositions, inserted in them what he had not preached, adjusting them maliciously, and sent them to one of his friends in Rome, to get them examined by the Sacred Congregation and by the Inquisition. At Rome they were pronounced good. That greatly disappointed and vexed him. After having been treated in this manner, and opprobriously reviled by him in the most offensive terms, Father La Combe, with much mildness and humility, told him he was going to Annecy, and if he had anything to write to the Bishop of Geneva, he would take care of his letter. He desired him to wait, as he was going to write. The good man had the patience to wait three hours, though he had treated him so exceedingly ill, as to snatch out of his hands a letter I had given him for Anselm. Hearing he was still in the church, I went to him and begged him to send and see if the other's packet was ready; because the day was so far gone he would be obliged to lodge by the way. When the messenger arrived, he found a servant of the ecclesiastic on horseback, ordered to go at full speed to Annecy before the father. He returned an answer that he had no letters to send by him. This was to gain time to prepossess the Bishop. Father La Combe then set off for Annecy, and on his arrival found the Bishop prepossessed and in ill humor. This was the substance of their discourse:

BISHOP.—You must engage this lady to give what she has to the house at Gex, and make her prioress.

F. LA COMBE.—You know what she has told you herself of her vocation, both at Paris and in this country. I do not believe she will engage, after quitting her all, in hope of entering Geneva. She has offered to stay with those sisters as a boarder, if they are willing she will remain; if not, she will retire into some convent, till God shall dispose of her otherwise.

BISHOP.—I know all that; but she is so obedient that, if you order her, she will assuredly do it.

F. LA COMBE.—For that reason one ought to be cautious in the commands laid on her. Can I induce a foreign lady, who has nothing but a pittance she has reserved to herself, to give that up in favor of a house not yet established, and perhaps never will be? If the house should fail, or be no longer of use, what shall that lady live on? Shall she go to the hospital?

BISHOP.—These reasons are good for nothing. If you do not make her do what I have said, I will degrade and suspend you.

This manner of speaking surprised the father, who understood the rules of suspension, which are not executed on such things. He replied:

"I am ready, not only to suffer the suspension, but even death, rather than do anything against my conscience." Then he retired.

He directly sent me this account by an express. I had no other course but to retire into the convent. I received a letter informing me that the nun to whom I had entrusted my daughter had fallen sick, and desiring me to go to her. I showed this letter to the sisters of our house, telling them I had a mind to go; but if they ceased to persecute me, and would leave Father La Combe in peace, I would return as soon as the mistress of my daughter recovered. Instead of this, they persecuted me more violently, wrote to Paris against me, stopped all my letters, and sent libels against me round the country.

The day after my arrival at Tonon, Father La Combe set off for the valley of Aoust. He had come to take leave of me, and told me he should go from thence to Rome, and perhaps not return. He was sorry to leave me in a strange country, without succor, and persecuted of everyone. I replied: "My father, that gives me no pain; I use the creatures for God, and by His order. Through His mercy, I do very well without them, when He withdraws them; and I am content never to see you, and to abide under persecution, if such be His will." He said he would go well satisfied to see me in such a disposition.

As soon as I got to the Ursulines, an aged pious priest, who for twenty years had not come out of his solitude, came to find me. He told me that he had a vision relative to me: a woman in a boat on the lake; and the Bishop of Geneva, with some of his priests, exerted all their efforts to sink the boat and drown her; that he continued in this vision above two hours, with pain of mind; that it seemed sometimes as if this woman were quite drowned, as she disappeared, but afterwards appeared again, ready to escape the danger, while the Bishop never ceased to pursue her. This woman was always calm, but he never saw her entirely free from him. From that he concluded that the Bishop would persecute me without intermission.

CHAPTER XX.

After Father La Combe was gone, the persecution became more violent. The Bishop of Geneva and his family had twenty-two intercepted letters, opened, on their table. In one was sent me a power of attorney to sign, of immediate consequence. They were obliged to put it under another cover, and send it to me. The Bishop wrote to Father de la Mothe. He declared against me. The Bishop made him his confidant. He spread abroad the news about me which they sent him. They imagined that I would annul the donation I had made, if I returned; that, having the support of friends in France, I would find the means of breaking it. They were mistaken; I had no thought of loving anything but the poverty of Jesus Christ.

I was in this convent, and had seen Father La Combe no further than I have mentioned, yet they did not cease to publish of him and me the most scandalous stories, as utterly false as anything could be, for he was a hundred and fifty leagues from me.

For some time I was ignorant of this. As I knew that all my letters were kept from me, I ceased to wonder at receiving none. I lived in this house with my little daughter in sweet repose and great favor of Providence.

When I was in my apartment, without any other director than our Lord by His Spirit, as soon as one of my little children came to knock at my door, He required me to admit the interruption. He showed me that it is not the actions in themselves which please Him, but the constant ready obedience to every discovery of His will, even in the minutest things, with such suppleness, as not to stick to anything, but still to turn with Him at every call. My soul was like a leaf, or a feather, which the wind moves what way soever it pleases; and the Lord never suffers a soul so dependent upon, and dedicated to Him, to be deceived.

Our Lord showed me, in a dream, two ways by which souls steer their course, under the figure of two drops of water. One of unparalleled beauty, brightness and purity; the other bright, yet full of little fibres. Both good to quench thirst; the former altogether pleasant, but the latter not so perfectly agreeable. By the former is represented the way of pure and naked faith, which pleases the Spouse much, it is so pure, so clear from all self-love. The way of emotions or gifts is not so; and yet in that, many enlightened souls walk, and in that they had drawn Father La Combe. But God showed me that He had given him to me, to draw him into one more pure and perfect. I spoke before the sisters, he being present, of the way of faith, how much more glorious it was to God, and advantageous for the soul, than all those gifts, emotions and assurances, which cause us to live to self. This discouraged them at first, and him also. I saw they were pained. I said no more. But, as he is a person of great humility, he bid me unfold what I had meant to say. I told him part of my dream of the two drops of water; yet he did not enter into what I said; but when he came to Gex, to make the retreats, our Lord made known to me, at prayer in the night, that I was his mother and he my son. I told him the circumstances of a certain time past; and he recollected that it was the time of so extraordinary a touch with which the Lord favored him that he was quite overwhelmed with contrition. This gave him such an interior renovation that, having retired to pray, in an ardent frame of mind, he was filled with joy, and seized with powerful emotion, which made him enter into what I had told him of the way of faith.

After Easter, in 1682, the Bishop came to Tonon. He then pressed me to return to Gex, and take the place of prioress. I gave him the reasons against it. I appealed to him, as a Bishop, desiring him to regard nothing but God. He was struck into confusion, and said: "Since you speak to me in such a manner, I can not advise you to it. It is not for us to go contrary to our vocations; but do good, I pray you, to this house." I promised him to do it; and having received my pension, I sent them a hundred pistoles, with a design of doing the same as long as I should be in the diocese.

My soul was in a state of entire resignation, and great content, in the midst of such violent tempests. Persons came to tell me extravagant stories against Father La Combe. The more they said the more esteem I felt for him. I answered them: "I may never see him again, but I shall be glad to do him justice. It is not he who hinders me from engaging at Gex. I know it to be none of my vocation." They asked me: "Who could know that better than the Bishop?" They told me that I was under a deception, and my state good for nothing. This gave me no uneasiness. A soul in this state seeks nothing for itself, but all for God. "What, then, does this soul?" It leaves itself to be conducted by God's providences. Outwardly, its life seems quite common; inwardly, it is wholly resigned to the Divine will. The more everything appears adverse and desperate, the more calm it is. It finds no more of that impurity which came from self-seeking, from a human manner of acting, from an unguarded word, from any warm emotion or eagerness. Though assaulted on every side, it continues fixed as a rock. Having no will but for what God sees meet to order, be it high or low, great or small, sweet or bitter, honor, wealth, life, or any other object, what can shake its peace?

Oh, if souls had courage to resign themselves to the work of purification, without having any weak and foolish pity on themselves, what rapid, happy progress would they make! But few are willing to lose the earth. If they advance some steps, as soon as the sea is ruffled they are dejected; they cast anchor, and often desist from the voyage. Such disorders doth selfish interest and self-love occasion. It is of consequence not to look too much at one's own state, not to lose courage, not to afford any nourishment to self-love, which is so deep-rooted that its empire is not easily demolished. Often the idea a man falsely conceives of the greatness of his advancement in divine experience makes him want it to be seen and known of men, and to wish to see the same perfection in others. He conceives too low ideas of others and too high of his own. Then it becomes a pain to him to converse with people too human; whereas, a soul truly mortified and resigned would rather converse with the worst, by the order of Providence, than with the best, of its own choice, wanting only to speak to any as Providence directs, knowing well that all beside, far from helping, only hurt or prove unfruitful.

What renders this soul so perfectly content? It neither knows, nor wants to know, anything but what God calls it to. Herein it enjoys divine content, vast, immense, and independent of exterior events; more satisfied in its humiliation, and in the opposition of all creatures, by the order of Providence, than on the throne of its own choice.

Here the apostolic life begins. Do all reach that state? Very few, as far as I can comprehend. There is a way of lights, gifts and graces, a holy life in which the creature appears all admirable. As this life is more apparent, so it is more esteemed of such as have not the purest light. The souls in the other path are often little known, for a length of time, as it was with Christ Himself, till the last of His life.

CHAPTER XXI.

I was told the ecclesiastic had won over the girl whom I loved. So strong a desire I had for her perfection it had cost me much. I should not have felt the death of a child so much as her loss. I was told how to hinder it, but that human way of acting was repugnant to my inward sense; and these words arose in my heart: "Except the Lord build the house" (Ps. cxxvii. 1).

And indeed He Himself hindered her from yielding to this deceitful man, after a manner to be admired. As long as I was with her she seemed wavering and fearful; but oh, the infinite goodness of God, to preserve without our aid what without His we should inevitably lose! I was no sooner separated from her, but she became immovable.

There scarcely passed a day but they treated me with new insults. The New Catholics, by the instigation of the Bishop of Geneva, the ecclesiastic, and the sisters at Gex, stirred up all the persons of piety against me. I had little uneasiness on my own account. If I could have had it at all, it would have been on account of Father La Combe, whom they vilely aspersed, though he was absent. At first I was too ready to vindicate him, thinking it justice. I did not do it at all for myself, and our Lord showed me that I must cease doing it for him, to leave him to be more thoroughly annihilated; from thence he would draw a greater glory than ever he had done from his own reputation.

Every day they invented some new slander. No kind of malicious device in their power did they omit.

They came to surprise and ensnare me in my words; but God guarded me so well they only discovered their own malevolence. I had no consolation from the creatures. She who had the care of my daughter behaved roughly to me. The maid I had brought, and who stayed with me, grew tired out. Wanting to go back again, she stunned me with her complaints, thwarting and chiding me from morning till night, upbraiding me with what I had left, and coming to a place where I was good for nothing. I was obliged to bear all her ill-humor and the clamor of her tongue.

My own brother, Father de la Mothe, wrote to me that I was a rebel to my Bishop, staying in his diocese only to give him pain. Father La Combe, at Rome, was received with much honor, and his doctrine highly esteemed.

About July, 1682, my sister, an Ursuline, got permission to come to the waters. She brought a maid with her, which was seasonable. My sister assisted in the education of my daughter, but she had frequent jarring with her tutoress. I labored in vain for peace. In this place, I saw clearly that it is not great gifts which sanctify, and death to everything is infinitely more beneficial; for one who thought herself at the summit of perfection has discovered since, by the trials which have befallen her, that she was far from it. Oh, how true it is that we may have of God's gifts, and be full of ourselves!

How straight is the gate which leads to a life in God! how little one must be to pass through it, it being nothing else but death to self! But when we have passed through it, what enlargement do we find! David saith (Psa. xviii. 19): "He brought me forth also into a large place." Through humiliation and abasement he was brought thither.

Father La Combe, on his arrival, came to see me. He said I must return. All seemed dark, and there was no likelihood that God would use me in this country. The Bishop of Geneva wrote to Father de la Mothe to get me to return, and he wrote to me to do it. The first Lent which I passed with the Ursulines, I had a great pain in my eyes; for the imposthume I formerly had between the eye and the nose returned three times. The bad air and noisome chamber contributed hereto. My head was frightfully swelled, but great was my inward joy. It was strange to see so many good creatures, who did not know me, love and pity me; and all the rest enraged against me, and most of them on reports entirely false, neither knowing me nor why they so hated me. To swell the stream of affliction my daughter fell sick and was likely to die. Her mistress also fell ill. My soul, leaving all to God, continued to rest in a quiet and peaceable habitation.

My daughter had the small-pox. They sent for a physician from Geneva, who gave her over. Father La Combe then came to pray with her. He gave her his blessing, and soon after she wonderfully recovered. The persecutions of the New Catholics against me increased, yet I did not fail to do them all the good in my power. Father La Combe regulated many things in regard to my daughter, which vexed her mistress so much that her friendship was turned to coldness. She had grace, but suffered nature to prevail. I told her of her faults, as I was inwardly directed; but though God enlightened her to see the truth, yet coldness towards me ensued. The debates between her and my sister grew more violent. My daughter, six years and a half old, by her little dexterities, found a way to please them both, choosing to do her exercises twice over, first with the one, then with the other, which continued not long; for as her mistress generally neglected her, doing things at one time and leaving them at another, she was reduced to learn only what my sister and I taught her. Indeed, the changeableness of my sister was so excessive that, without great grace, it was hard to suit one's self to it. Formerly, I could scarce bear her manners; but I have since loved everything in God, who has given me great facility to bear the faults of my neighbor, with a readiness to please and oblige everyone, and such a compassion for their distresses as I never had before.

I have no difficulty to use condescension with imperfect persons; I should be secretly smitten if I failed therein; but with souls of grace I can not suffer long and frequent conversations. It is a thing few are capable of. Some religious persons say these conversations are of great service. It may be true for some, but not for all; for there is a period wherein it hurts, especially when it is of our own choice, the human inclination corrupting everything. The same things which would be profitable when God, by His Spirit, draws to them, become quite otherwise when we of ourselves enter into them. I prefer being a whole day with the worst of persons in obedience to God, before being one hour with the best, from my own choice and inclination.

The order of Divine Providence makes the whole rule of a soul entirely devoted to God. While it faithfully gives itself up thereto, it will do all things right and well, and have everything it wants, without its own care; because God in whom it confides, makes it every moment do what He requires, and furnishes the occasion for it. God loves what is of His own order and His own will, not according to the idea of the rational or even enlightened man; for He hides these persons from the eyes of others, to preserve them in that hidden purity for Himself.

How comes it that such souls commit any faults? Because they are not faithful, in giving themselves up to the present moment. Too eagerly bent on something, or wanting to be over-faithful, they slide into faults they can neither foresee nor avoid. Does God, then, leave souls which confide in Him? Surely not. Sooner would He work a miracle to hinder them from falling, if they were resigned enough to Him. They may be resigned as to the general will, and fail as to the present moment. Being out of the order of God, they fall. They renew such falls as long as they continue out of Divine order. When they return into it, all goes right and well.

Most assuredly if such souls were faithful enough, not to let any of the moments of the order of God slip over, they would not thus fall. As a dislocated bone out of the place of Divine wisdom gives continual pain till restored to its proper order, so many troubles come from the soul not abiding in its place, and not being content with the order of God, from moment to moment. If men rightly knew this secret, they would be fully content and satisfied. But alas! instead of being content with what they have, they are ever wishing for what they have not; while the soul which enters into the Divine light begins to be in paradise. What makes paradise? The order of God, which renders all the saints infinitely content, though unequal in glory!

All souls have more or less of ardent desires, except those whose will is lost in the will of God. Some have good desires to suffer martyrdom; others thirst for the salvation of their neighbor, and some pant to see God in glory. All this is excellent. But he who rests in the

Divine will, although he may be exempt from all these desires, is infinitely more content and glorifies God more. It is written concerning Jesus Christ, when He drove out of the temple those who profaned it: "The zeal of thine house hath eaten me up" (John ii. 17). It was in that moment of the order of God, that these words had their effect. How many times had Jesus Christ been in the temple without such conduct? Does not He occasionally say of Himself, that His hour was not yet come?

CHAPTER XXII.

Father La Combe returned from Rome, well approved, and furnished with testimonials of his life and doctrine. I gave him an account of what I had suffered, and what care God had taken of all my concerns. I saw His providence incessantly extended to the smallest things. After having been several months without any news of my papers, when some pressed me to write and blamed my neglect, an invisible Hand held me back; my peace and confidence were great herein. I received a letter from the ecclesiastic at home, which informed me he had orders to come and see me, and bring me my papers. I had sent to Paris for a bundle of things for my daughter. I heard they were lost on the lake. But I gave myself no trouble. The man who had taken the charge of them made a search a whole month, without any news about them. At the end of three months they were brought to me, having been found in the house of a poor man, who had not opened them, nor knew who had brought them there. Once I sent for all the money which was to serve me a whole year; the person who had been to receive cash for the bill of exchange, having put that money in two bags on horseback, forgot that it was there, and gave the horse to a little boy to lead. The money fell from the horse in the market at Geneva. That instant I arrived, coming on the other side, and having alighted from my litter, the first thing I found was my money, in walking over it. A great throng was in this place, and not one had perceived it. Many such things attended me, which, to avoid prolixity, I pass by. These suffice to show the continual protection of God.

The Bishop of Geneva continued to persecute me. To relieve myself from the fatigue of continual conversation, as my body grew weak, I desired Father La Combe to allow me a retreat. Then I let myself be consumed by love all the day long. Then I perceived the quality of a spiritual mother; for the Lord gave me what I can not express for the perfection of souls. This I could not hide from Father La Combe. It seemed to me I entered into the inmost recesses of his heart. Our Lord showed me he was His servant, chosen among a thousand, that He would lead him through total death, and the entire destruction of the old man; that He would have me instrumental to cause him to walk in the way in which He had led me first, that I might be in a condition to direct others therein, and tell them the way through which I have passed; that the Lord would have us to become one in Him; that though my soul was more advanced now, yet he should one day pass beyond it, with a bold and rapid flight. God knows how I rejoiced herein, and with what joy I would see my spiritual children surpass their mother in glory.

In this retreat I felt a strong propensity to write, but resisted it till I fell sick. I had nothing to write about, not one idea. It was a Divine impulse, with such fulness of grace as was hard to contain. I told Father La Combe. He answered he had a strong impulse to command me to write, but had not dared on account of my weakness. I told him that weakness was the effect of my resistance, and would, through my writing, go off. He ordered me to write. I knew not the first word I should write; but when I began, matter flowed impetuously, and I was relieved and grew better. I wrote a treatise on the interior path of faith, under the comparison of torrents, streams and rivers; and though it is long, the comparison holds to the end.

As the way God now conducted Father La Combe was different from that in which he had formerly walked, which had been all light, knowledge, ardor, assurance, sentiment; but now the poor, low, despised path of faith and nakedness, he found it hard to submit, which caused me no little suffering.

The possession the Lord had of my soul became every day stronger, so that I passed days without being able to pronounce one word; for the Lord was pleased to make me pass wholly into Him by an entire internal transformation. He became the absolute Master of my heart, to such a degree as not to leave me a movement of my own, that I might be continually supple to every intimation of His will. This state did not hinder me from condescending to my sister and the others, but the useless things with which they were taken up could not interest me. That induced me to ask leave to make a retreat, to let myself be possessed of Him who holds me so closely united to Himself after an ineffable manner.

I had so ardent a desire for the perfection of Father La Combe, and to see him thoroughly die to himself, that I could have wished him all the crosses imaginable, that might conduce to this blessed end. Whenever he was unfaithful, or looked at things in any other light than this death of self, I felt myself on the rack, which surprised me. To the Lord I made my complaint, who graciously encouraged me.

My sister had brought me a maid, whom God was willing to give me, to fashion her according to His will, not without crucifixion to myself; for I believe it never is to fall out that our Lord will give me any persons without my suffering for them, whether to draw them into a spiritual life, or never to leave me without the cross. She was one on whom the Lord had conferred singular graces. She passed for a saint. Our Lord brought her to me, to let her see the difference between sanctity comprised in those gifts with which she was endowed, and that obtained by our entire destruction, even by the loss of those gifts, and all that raised us in the esteem of men.

This girl fell grievously sick. I found I had nothing to do but command her bodily sickness, or the disposition of her mind, and all I said was done. Then I learned what it was to command by the Word, and obey by the Word. It was Jesus Christ in me equally commanding and obeying.

One day, after dinner, I was moved to say to her: "Rise and be no longer sick." She arose and was cured. The nuns were much astonished; and as they knew nothing of what had passed, but saw her walking who in the morning had appeared to be in the last extremity, they attributed her disorder to a vivid imagination.

I have experienced how much God respects the freedom of man, and even demands his free concurrence; for when I said, "Be healed," or, "Be free from your troubles," if such persons acquiesced, the Word was efficacious, and they were healed. If they resisted or doubted, though under fair pretexts, as, "I shall be healed when it pleases God," or, "I can not be healed," then the Word had no effect, and the Divine virtue retired in me. I experienced what our Lord said, when the woman afflicted with the issue of blood touched Him, and He asked: "Who touched me?" The apostles said: "Master, the multitude throng thee, . . and sayest thou,

Who touched me?" But He replied: "Virtue is gone out of me" (Luke viii. 45, 46). Jesus Christ caused that healing virtue to flow through me by means of His Word; but when that virtue met not with a correspondence in the subject, I felt it suspended in its source, which gave me pain. One can not conceive the delicacy of this healing virtue. Though it has much power over things inanimate, the least thing in man restrains it or stops it.

A good nun much afflicted, and under a violent temptation, went to declare her case to a sister whom she thought spiritual, and in a condition capable of assisting her. But far from finding succor, she was discouraged and cast down. The other despised and repulsed her, and treating her with contempt and rigor, said: "Don't come near me, since you are that way." This poor girl in distress came to me, thinking herself undone. I consoled her, and our Lord relieved her immediately. The sister who had used her in such a manner came also to me, highly pleased with herself, saying she abhorred such tempted creatures; that she was proof against such temptations, and never had a bad thought. I said to her: "My sister, from the friendship I have for you I wish you the pain of her who spoke to you, and one still more violent." She answered haughtily: "If you were to ask it from God for me, and I ask of Him the contrary, I believe I shall be heard as soon as you." I answered: "If it be only my own interests which I ask, I shall not be heard; but if it be those of God only I shall be heard sooner than you are aware." That very night she fell into violent temptation, and continued in it a fortnight. She had ample occasion to acknowledge her own weakness, and what she would be without grace. She conceived a violent hatred for me, saying I was the cause of her pain, but soon saw what had brought on her so terrible a state.

I fell sick, even to extremity. Several times I saw in dreams Father de la Mothe raising persecutions against me. Our Lord let me know this would be the case, and Father La Combe would forsake me in the time of persecution. It has since been found true; though not with his will, but from necessity, having been himself persecuted the first. He was to preach during Lent. People came five leagues to pass several days there for the benefit of his ministry. I heard he was so sick he was like to die, and prayed the Lord to restore his health. My prayer was heard and he soon recovered.

During my extraordinary sickness, which continued six months, the Lord gradually taught me there was another manner of conversing among souls wholly His, than by speech. I learned a language before unknown. When Father La Combe entered, I could speak no more; and there was formed in my soul the same kind of silence to him as to God. God was willing to show me that men might learn the language of angels. I was gradually reduced to speak to him only in silence. Then we understood each other in God, after a manner unutterable and all divine. Our hearts spoke to each other, communicating a grace no words can express. It was like a new country, both for him and for me, so divine that I can not describe it. God penetrated us with Himself in a manner so pure, so sweet, that we passed hours in this profound silence, always communicative, without being able to utter one word. He learned, by experience, the operations of the heavenly Word to reduce souls into unity with itself, and what purity one may arrive at in this life. It was given me to communicate this way to other good souls, but with this difference, that I did nothing but communicate to them in this sacred silence an extraordinary strength and grace, but I received nothing from them; whereas with Father La Combe there was a flow and return of communication of grace, which he received from me, and I from him, in the greatest purity.

In this long malady the love of God, and of Him alone, made up my whole occupation. I seemed so entirely lost in Him as to have no sight of myself. It seemed as if my heart never came out of that divine ocean, having been drawn into it through deep humiliations.

Jesus was living in me; I lived no more. These words were imprinted in me, as a real state into which I must enter: "The foxes have holes, and the birds of the air have nests; but the Son of man hath not where to lay his head" (Matt. viii. 20). This I have since experienced in all its extent, having no sure abode, no refuge among my friends, who were ashamed of me, and openly renounced me, nor among my relations, most of whom declared themselves my adversaries, and were my greatest persecutors; while others looked on me with contempt and indignation. "For Thy sake I have borne reproach; shame hath covered my face. I am become a stranger unto my brethren, and an alien unto my mother's children" (Psa. lxix. 7, 8).

He showed me all the world in a rage against me, without any one daring to appear for me, and assured me in the ineffable silence of His eternal Word, that He would give me vast numbers of children, which I should bring forth by the cross. I left it to Him to do with me whatever He pleased, esteeming my whole and sole interest to be placed entirely in His Divine Will. He gave me to see how the devil was going to stir up an outrageous persecution against prayer, yet it should prove the means God would use to establish it. He gave me to see how He would guide me into the wilderness, to be nourished for a time. The wings to bear me thither were the resignation of my whole self to His holy will, and the love of the same will. I think I am at present in that wilderness, separated from the whole world in my imprisonment; and I see already accomplished in part what was shown me.

In this sickness I was often at the point of death. I fell into convulsions from violent pains. Father La Combe administered the sacrament to me. I was well satisfied to die, as was he also in the expectation of my departure. For, united in God after a manner so pure and so spiritual, death could not separate us. Father La Combe, on his knees at my bedside, remarking how my eyes faded, seemed ready to give me up, when God inspired him to lift up his hands, and with a strong voice, heard by all in my chamber, almost full, to command death to relinquish its hold. Thus God was pleased wonderfully to raise me up again. For a long time I continued weak. Our Lord still gave me new testimonies of His love. How many times was He pleased to make use of His servant to restore me to life, when I was on the point of expiring! They judged the air of the lake on which the convent was situated was prejudicial to my constitution, and that it would be necessary for me to remove.

Our Lord put it into the heart of Father La Combe to establish a hospital in this place for the poor people seized with maladies, and to institute also a committee of ladies to furnish such as could not leave their families to go to the hospital, with the means of subsistence during their illness, after the manner of France. Willingly did

I enter into it; and without any other fund than Providence we began it. We dedicated it to the holy Child Jesus, and He was pleased to give the first beds to it from the earnest-pence of my pension, which belong to Him. In a short time there were nearly twelve beds in it, and three persons of great piety gave themselves without salary to the service of the poor patients. I supplied them with ointments and medicines, freely given to the poor people of the town who had need of them. All these things, which cost little, and owed all their success to the blessing God gave, drew upon us new persecutions. The Bishop of Geneva was offended more than ever, seeing these small matters rendered me beloved. He said I won over everybody. He openly declared that he could not bear me in his diocese. He extended the persecution to the women who had been my assistants.

My sister was weary of this house, and as soon as the season for the waters approached, they took occasion from thence to send her away with the maid I had brought, who had molested me exceedingly in my late illness.

While I was yet indisposed, the Ursulines, with the Bishop of Verceil, earnestly requested the Father-General of the Barnabites to seek among the religious a man of merit, piety and learning, who might serve him for a prebend and a counsellor. He cast his eyes on Father La Combe; yet before he absolutely engaged him with the Bishop, he wrote to him, to know whether he had any objection. Father La Combe replied that he had no other will but that of obeying him, and he might command him herein as he should think best. He gave me an account of this, and that we were going to be entirely separated. I was glad our Lord would employ him under a Bishop who knew him, and would be likely to do him justice.

CHAPTER XXIII.

I then went from the Ursulines, and they sought for a house for me at a distance from the lake. There was but one empty, of the greatest poverty. It had no chimney but in the kitchen, through which one must pass to go to the chamber. I took my daughter with me, and gave up the largest chamber for her and her maid. I was lodged in a little hole, on straw, to which I went up by a ladder. As we had no other furniture but our beds, plain and homely, I bought some straw chairs and Dutch earthen and wooden ware. Never did I enjoy a greater content than in this little hole, so conformable to the state of Jesus Christ. I fancied everything better on wood than on silver plate. I laid in provisions, hoping to stay there a long time, but the devil did not leave me long in such sweet peace. It would be difficult for me to tell the persecutions against me. They threw stones in my windows, which fell at my feet. They came in the night, tore up my little garden, broke down the arbor, and overturned everything, as if ravaged by soldiers. They came to abuse me at the door all night long, making such a racket as if they were going to break it open.

Though I continued my charities at Gex, I was not the less persecuted. They offered one person a warrant to compel Father La Combe to stay at Tonon, thinking he would otherwise be a support to me in the persecution, but we prevented it. I knew not then the designs of God, and that He would soon draw me from that poor solitary place, in which I enjoyed a sweet and solid satisfaction, notwithstanding the abuses from without. I thought myself happier here than any sovereign on earth. It was for me like a nest; and Christ was willing that I should be like Him. The devil irritated my persecutors. They sent to desire me to go out of the diocese. All the good which the Lord had caused me to do in it was condemned, more than the greatest crimes. Crimes were tolerated; me they could not endure.

It was therefore concluded that Father La Combe should conduct me to Turin, and go from thence to Verceil.

I took with me a religious man of merit, who had taught theology for fourteen years, to take away from our enemies all cause for slander. I also took a boy I had brought out of France. They hired a carriage for my daughter, my chambermaid and myself. But all precautions are useless, when it pleases God to permit them to be frustrated. Our adversaries immediately wrote to Paris I was gone alone with Father La Combe, strolling about the country from province to province, with many such fables, weak and wicked. We suffered all with patience, without vindicating ourselves, or making complaint.

Scarcely were we arrived at Turin, but the Bishop of Geneva wrote against us. Father La Combe repaired to Verceil, and I stayed at Turin, with the Marchioness of Prunai. But what crosses from my own family, the Bishop of Geneva, the Barnabites, and a vast number of persons besides! My eldest son came to find me out, on the death of my mother-in-law, an augmentation of my troubles; but after we heard his accounts of things, and how they had sold all the moveables, chosen guardians, and settled every article, without consulting me, I seemed entirely useless. Yet it was judged not proper for me to return, considering the rigor of the season.

The Marchioness of Prunai, who had been so warmly desirous of my company, seeing my great crosses, looked coldly upon me. My childlike simplicity, the state wherein God kept me, passed for stupidity, though in that condition He inspired me to utter oracles. For when the question was to help anyone, or about anything which God required of me, He gave me, with the weakness of a child, tokens of Divine strength. Her heart was quite shut up to me. Our Lord, however, made me foretell events which since that time have actually been fulfilled, to herself, her daughter, and the virtuous ecclesiastic who lived at her house. She did not fail at last to conceive more friendship for me, seeing Christ in me. Self-love and fear of reproach had closed her heart. She thought her state more advanced than it was by reason of her being without tests; but she soon saw by experience I had told her the truth. She was obliged for family reasons to leave Turin, and live on her own estate. She solicited me to go with her; but the education of my daughter did not permit. To stay at Turin without her seemed improper, because, having lived retired in this place, I made no acquaintance in it. I knew not which way to turn.

During my residence at Turin, our Lord conferred on me great favors. I found myself every day more transformed into Him, and had continually more knowledge of the state of souls, without ever being mistaken or deceived therein. When I told Father La Combe about the state of some souls, which appeared to him more advanced than the knowledge given to me of them, he attributed it to pride. He was angry with me, and prejudiced. I had no uneasiness on account of his esteeming me the less. He could not reconcile my willing obedience in most things, with so extraordinary a firmness. He admitted a distrust of my grace; for he did not comprehend that it did not in any wise depend on me to be one way or another; and that if I had any such power, I should have suited myself to what he said, to spare myself the crosses my firmness caused me, or would have artfully dissembled my real sentiments. I could do neither. Were all to perish by it, I was constrained to tell him just as our Lord directed me. In this He has given me an inviolable fidelity to the last. No crosses have ever made me fail a moment therein. These things, which appeared the strong prejudice of a conceited opinion, set him against me. And though he tried to conceal it, yet how far distant soever he were, I could not be ignorant of it; my spirit felt it more or less, as the opposition was stronger or weaker; and as soon as it abated or ended my pain ceased. He also experienced the like. He told me many times: "When I stand well with God, I am well with you. When I am otherwise with Him, I find myself to be so with you." Thus he saw that when God received him into His bosom, it was always in uniting him to me, as if He would accept of nothing from him but in this union.

One night in a dream our Lord showed me He would purify the maid He had given me, and make her truly enter into death to herself. I then resolved to suffer for her, as I did for Father La Combe. As she resisted God much more than he, and was much more under the power of self-love, she had more to be purified from. The devil can not hurt us but so far as we retain some fondness for this corrupt self. God gave me the discerning of spirits, which would ever accept what was from Him, or reject what was not; not from any common methods of judging, or outward information, but by an inward principle which is His gift alone.

People often think they have discernment, when it is nothing but sympathy or antipathy of nature. Our Lord had destroyed in me every sort of natural antipathy. The soul must be pure, and depending on God alone, that all these things may be experienced in Him. In proportion as this maid became inwardly purified, my pain abated, till the Lord let me know her state was going to be changed, which soon ensued. In comparison of inward pain for souls, outward persecutions, though ever so violent, scarce gave me any.

The Bishop of Geneva wrote in my favor to different persons, whom he thought would show me his letters, and quite the contrary in the letters he thought I would never see. These persons, having showed each other the letters from him, were struck with indignation to see so shameful a duplicity. They sent me those letters, that I might take proper precautions. I kept them two years, and burnt them, not to hurt the prelate by them. The strongest battery he raised against me was what he did with the Secretary of State, who held that post in conjunction with the Marchioness of Prunai's brother. He used all imaginable endeavors to render me odious. He employed certain abbots for that purpose, so that, though I appeared little abroad, I was known by the descriptions this Bishop had given of me. This did not make so much impression as it would have done, if he had appeared in a better light at Court. Some letters of his her royal highness found after the prince's death, written to him against her, had that effect on the princess, that, instead of taking any notice of what he now wrote against me, she showed me great respect, and sent her request for me to come to see her. Accordingly, I waited on her. She assured me of her protection, and that she was glad of my being in her dominions.

It pleased God here to make use of me to the conversion of ecclesiastics. But I had much to suffer from their repugnances and infidelities—one of whom had villified me greatly—and even after his conversion turned aside into his old ways; but God graciously restored him.

As I was undetermined whether I should place my daughter at the Visitation of Turin, or take some other course, I was exceedingly surprised to see Father La Combe arrive from Verceil, and tell me I must return to Paris without any delay. It was in the evening, and he said I must set off the next morning. This sudden news startled me. It was a double sacrifice to return to a place where they had cried me down so much, and towards a family which held me in contempt. Behold me then disposed to go off, without offering a single word in reply, with my daughter and my maid, without anybody to guide us; for Father La Combe was resolved not to accompany me, because the Bishop of Geneva had written that I was gone to Turin to run after him. But the Father Provincial, a man of quality, and well acquainted with the virtue of Father La Combe, told him it was improper and unsafe for me to venture on these mountains, without some person of my acquaintance; and ordered him to accompany me to Grenoble, and from thence return to Turin. I went off then for Paris, there to suffer whatever crosses it should please God to inflict.

What made me pass Grenoble was the desire to spend a few days with a lady, an eminent servant of God. When I was there Father La Combe and that lady spoke to me not to go any farther; that God would glorify

Himself by me in that place. He returned and I left myself to be conducted by Providence. This lady took me to the house of a good widow. I placed my daughter in a convent. I made no visit in this place, but was greatly surprised when there came to me several persons who made profession of a singular devotion to God. I perceived a gift He had given me. I felt myself invested with the apostolic state, and discerned the conditions of such persons as spoke to me, and that with so much facility, that they were surprised and said that I gave them the thing they stood in need of. It was Thou, O my God, who didst all these things! From six in the morning till eight in the evening I was taken up in speaking of the Lord. People flocked on all sides, far and near, friars, priests, men of the world, maids, wives, widows, all came one after another; and the Lord supplied me with what was satisfactory to them all, after a wonderful manner, without any share of my meditation therein. Nothing was hid from me of what passed within them. I had not a syllable to say to such as came only to watch my words and criticise them. Even when I thought to try to speak to them I could not. God would not have me do it. Some of them said: "The people are fools to go to see that lady. She can not speak." Others treated me as if I were a stupid simpleton. After they left there came one and said: "I could not get hither soon enough to apprise you not to speak to those persons; they come to try what they can catch from you to your disadvantage." I answered them: "I was not able to say one word to them." Amidst this general applause, our Lord made me comprehend that to give one's self up to the help of souls, in the purity of His Spirit, was to expose one's self to the most cruel persecutions. These words were printed on my heart: "'To resign ourselves to serve our neighbor is to sacrifice ourselves to a gibbet. Such as now proclaim, 'Blessed is he who cometh in the name of the Lord,' will soon cry out, 'Away with him, crucify him.'" One of my friends speaking of the general esteem the people had for me, I said: "You will hear curses out of the same mouths which at present pronounce blessings." Our Lord made me comprehend that I must be conformable to Him in all His states; and that, if He had continued in a private life with His parents, He never had been crucified; that, when He would resign any of His servants to crucifixion, He employed such in the service of their neighbors. All the souls truly in the apostolic state are to suffer extremely. I speak not of those who put themselves into it; not being called of God, and having nothing of the grace of the apostleship, have none of its crosses; but of those only who surrender themselves to God, willing with their whole hearts to be exposed, for His sake, to sufferings without any mitigation.

CHAPTER XXIV.

Among so great a number of good souls, on whom our Lord wrought much by me, some were given me only as plants to cultivate. I knew their state, but had not that near connection with, or authority over them, which I had over others.

I never in all my life had so much consolation as to see in this little town so many pious souls who with a heavenly emulation gave up their whole hearts to God. There were girls of twelve who industriously followed their work almost all the day in silence, and in their employments enjoyed a communion with God. As these girls were poor, they placed themselves two and two together, and such as could do it read to others who could not. One saw the innocence of the primitive Christians revived. There was a poor laundress who had five children, and a husband paralytic, yet worse distempered in mind than in body. He had little strength left for anything else than to beat her. Yet this poor woman bore it with all meekness and patience, while she by her labor supported him and his five children. She had a wonderful gift of prayer, and amidst her great suffering and extreme poverty, preserved the presence of God and tranquility of mind. There was also a shop-keeper, and one who made locks, much affected with God. These were close friends. Sometimes the one and sometimes the other read to this laundress; and they were surprised to find that she was instructed by the Lord Himself in all they read to her, and spoke divinely of it.

Those friars sent for this woman, and threatened her if she did not leave off prayer, telling her it was only for churchmen to pray. She replied Christ had commanded all to pray, without specifying either priests or friars; that without prayer she could not support her crosses and poverty; that formerly she had lived without it and was very wicked; that since she had been in the exercise of it, she had loved God with all her soul; so that to leave off prayer was to renounce her salvation, which she could not do. Such words from such a woman one would think might have fully convinced them; but it only irritated them the more. They assured her she should have no absolution till she promised them to desist from prayer. She said: "Christ is Master of what He communicates to His creatures, and can do with it what He pleases." They refused her absolution, and after railing at a good tailor who served God with his whole heart, they ordered all the books which treated on prayer to be brought to them, and burned them with their own hands in the public square. They were much elated, but all the town arose in an uproar on account of the late insolent and intolerable abuse of the father of the oratory. The principal men went to the Bishop of Geneva, and complained to him of the scandals of these new missionaries, so different from the others. Speaking of Father La Combe, who had been there before them on his mission, they said these seemed sent to destroy all the good he had done. The Bishop was forced to come to that town and mount the pulpit, protesting he had no share in it, and these fathers had pushed their zeal too far. The friars declared they had done all they did pursuant to the orders given them.

It was the friars of this very order whom our Lord made use of to establish prayer in many places. And where they went they carried a hundred times more books of prayer than those their brethren burned.

One day when I was sick, a brother who had skill in curing diseases, came for a charitable collection, but hearing I was ill came in to see me, and gave me medicines for my disorder. We entered into a conversation which revived in him the love he had for God, which he acknowledged had been too much stifled by his great occupations. Our Lord conferred on him many favors, and gave him to be one of my true children.

Before I arrived at Grenoble, my friend there saw in a dream that our Lord gave me an infinite number of children all uniformly clad, bearing on their habits the marks of candor and innocence. She thought I was coming to take care of the children of the hospital. But as soon as she told me, I discerned it was not that which the dream meant; but that our Lord would give me, by a spiritual fruitfulness, a great number of children.

The physician of whom I have spoken was disposed to lay open his heart to me like a child. Our Lord gave him through me all that was necessary for him.

He brought me some of his companions who were friars; and the Lord took hold of them all. It was at the same time the other friars were making all the ravages I have mentioned. I could not but admire to see how the Lord was pleased to make amends for former damages, by pouring out His Spirit in abundance on these men, while the others were laboring vehemently against it.

But those good souls, instead of being staggered by persecutions, grew the stronger by it. The Superior, and the master of the novices of the house in which this doctor was, declared against me, without knowing me; and were grievously chagrined that a woman should be so much sought after. Looking at things as they were in themselves, and not as they were in the Lord, they had contempt for the gift which was lodged in so mean an instrument, instead of esteeming the Lord and His grace. This physician at length got the Superior to come and thank me for the good I had done them. Our Lord so ordered that he found something in my conversation which took hold of him. He was completely brought over. And he, sometime after, being visitor, dispersed a number of those books, bought at their own charge, which the others had tried to destroy.

There were in this noviciate many novices. The eldest of them grew uneasy under his vocation. So great was his trouble that he could neither read, study, pray, nor do scarcely any of his duties. His companion brought him to me. The Lord discovered to me the cause of his disorder and its remedy. I told it to him; and he began to practice prayer, even that of the heart. He was wonderfully changed. He felt relieved of his pain before he left the room. He then readily, joyfully, and perfectly studied and prayed, and discharged all his duties in such a manner, that he was scarce known to himself or others. What astonished him most was a remarkable gift of prayer. He gradually brought me all the novices, all of whom partook the effects of grace, though differently, according to their different temperaments. Never was there a more flourishing noviciate.

The master and Superior could not forbear admiring so great a change in their novices, though they did not know the cause. One day, as they were speaking of it to the collector, he said to them: "It is the lady against whom you have exclaimed so much without knowing her, whom God has made use of for all this." They were much surprised; and both the master and his

Superior submitted humbly to practice prayer, after the manner taught by a little book which the Lord inspired me to write. They reaped such benefit from it, that the Superior said to me: "I am become quite a new man. I could not practice prayer before, because my reasoning faculty was grown dull and exhausted; but now I do it as often as I will, with ease, with much fruit, and a quite different sensation of the presence of God." And the master said: "I have been a friar these forty years, and can truly say that I never knew how to pray, nor have I ever known or tasted of God, as I have done since I read that little book."

Many others were gained to God, whom I looked on to be my true children. He gave me three famous friars, of an order by which I have been, and still am, much persecuted. He made me also of service to a great number of nuns, virtuous young women, men of the world, priests, friars, three curates, one canon, and one grand-vicar.

There was one daughter given me, whom our Lord made use of to gain many others to Him. She was in a strange state of death when I first saw her, and He gave her life and peace. She afterwards fell extremely ill. The doctors said she would die; but I had an assurance of the contrary, and that God would make use of her to gain souls.

A sister in a monastery had been for eight years in a deep melancholy, unrelieved by anyone. Her director increased it by remedies contrary to her disorder. I had never been in that monastery. At eight o'clock at night one came for me. She had gone to such excess, that she had taken a knife to kill herself; but the knife fell out of her hand, and a person coming to see her had advised her to speak to me. Our Lord made me know what the matter was, and that He required her to resign herself to Him, instead of resisting Him as they had made her do for eight years. She entered at once into a peace of paradise; all her pains and troubles were instantly banished, and never returned. She has the greatest capacity of any in the house. She was presently so changed as to be the admiration of the whole community. Our Lord gave her a great gift of prayer and His continual presence, with a faculty and readiness for everything. A domestic also, who had troubled her for twenty-two years past, was delivered from her troubles, and is become a religious woman. That produced a close tie of friendship between the prioress and me, as the wonderful change in this sister surprised her, she having so often seen her in terrible sorrow. I also contracted other ties in this monastery.

I was specially moved to read the Holy Scriptures. When I began I was impelled to write the passage, and instantly its explication was given me, which I also wrote, going on with inconceivable expedition. Before I wrote I knew not what I was going to write. And after I had written, I remembered nothing of what I had penned, nor could I make use of it for the help of souls; but the Lord gave me, at the time I spoke to them, without any reflection, all that was necessary. Thus the Lord made me go on with an explanation of the holy, internal sense of the Scriptures. I had no other book but the Bible. Writing on the Old Testament, I made use of passages of the New without seeking them; they were given me along with the explication; and in writing on the New Testament, and therein making use of passages of the Old, they were given me in like manner. I had scarce any time for writing but in the night, allowing only one or two hours to sleep. The Lord made me write with so much purity, that I was obliged to leave off or begin again, as He was pleased to order. He proved me every way herein. When I wrote by day, often suddenly interrupted, I left the word unfinished, and He afterwards gave me what He pleased. If I gave way to reflection I was punished for it, and could not proceed. Sometimes I was not duly attentive to the Divine Spirit, thinking I did well to continue when I had time, even without feeling His immediate impulse or enlightening influence, from whence it is easy to see some place clear and consistent, and others which have neither taste nor unction; such is the difference of the Spirit of God from the natural spirit.

Methinks the Lord acts with His dearest friends as the sea with its waves. Sometimes it pushes them against the rocks where they break in pieces; sometimes it rolls them on the sand, or dashes them on the mire, then instantly it retakes them into the depths of its own bosom, where they are absorbed with the same rapidity that they were first ejected. Even among the good the far greater part are souls only of mercy; and that is well, but to appertain to Divine justice, oh, how rare and yet how great! Mercy is distributive in favor of the creature, but justice destroys everything of the creature, without sparing anything.

My particular friend began to conceive some jealousy on the applause given me, God permitting it for the farther purification of her soul, through this weakness, and the pain it caused her. Also some confessors began to be uneasy, saying it was none of my business to invade their province, and meddle in the help of souls; and that some of the penitents had a great affection for me. It was easy to see the difference between those confessors who, in their conducting of souls, seek nothing but God, and those who seek themselves therein; for the first came to see me, and rejoiced greatly at the grace of God bestowed on their penitents, without fixing their attention on the instrument. The others tried to stir up the town against me. Two friars came, one of them a man of profound learning and a great preacher. They came separately, after having studied a number of difficult things to propose to me. But though they were matters far out of my reach, the Lord made me answer as if I had studied them all my life; after which I spoke to them as He inspired me. They went away convinced and satisfied, affected with the love of God.

I still continued writing with a prodigious swiftness; for the hand could scarcely follow fast enough the Spirit which dictated. The transcriber could not copy in five days what I wrote in one night. Whatever is good in it comes from God only. Whatever is otherwise, from myself. In the day I had scarcely time to eat, by reason of the vast numbers of people which came thronging to me. I wrote the Canticles in a day and a half, and received several visits besides.

A considerable part of the book of Judges was lost. Being desired to render that book complete, I wrote over again the places lost. Afterwards they were found. My former and latter explications were found to be perfectly conformable to each other, which greatly surprised persons of knowledge and merit, who attested the truth of it.

A counsellor of the parlament, a servant of God, finding on my table a tract on prayer, I had written long before, desired me to lend it. He lent it to friends to whom he thought it might be of service. Everyone wanted copies of it. He resolved to have it printed. They requested me to write a preface, and thus was that little book printed, which has since made so much noise, and been the pretence for the several persecutions. This counsellor was one of my intimate friends, and a pattern of piety. The book has passed through five editions; and our Lord has given a great benediction to it. Those good friars took fifteen hundred of them.

CHAPTER XXV.

A poor girl of great simplicity, who earned her livelihood by her labor, and was inwardly favored of the Lord, came all sorrowful to me, and said: "Oh, my mother, I have seen you like a lamb in the midst of a vast troop of furious wolves. I have seen a frightful multitude of people of all ranks and robes, of all ages, sexes and conditions, priests, frairs, married men, maids and wives, with pikes, halberts and drawn swords, all eager for your instant destruction. You let them alone without stirring or being surprised. I looked on all sides to see whether anyone would come to defend you, but I saw not one." Some days after, those who through envy were raising private batteries against me broke forth. Envious people wrote against me, without knowing me. They said I was a sorceress; that it was by a magic power I attracted souls; that everything in me was diabolical; that if I did some charities, it was because I coined and put off false money, with many other gross accusations.

As the tempest increased, the Bishop of Grenoble's Almoner persuaded me to go to Marseilles, to let the storm pass over, telling me I would be well received there, it being his native soil. I wrote to Father La Combe for his consent. He readily gave it. I might have gone to Verceil, for the Bishop of Verceil had written earnestly pressing me to come thither. But a human respect, and a fear of affording a handle to my enemies, gave me an extreme aversion thereto.

Besides, the Marchioness of Prunai, who, since my

departure from her, had been more enlightened by her own experience, having met with a part of the things which I thought would befall her, had conceived for me a strong friendship and intimate union of spirit. No two sisters could be more united than we were. She was extremely desirous that I would return to her, as I had formerly promised. But I could not resolve upon this, lest it should be thought that I was gone after Father La Combe. But, O my God, how was this relic of self-love overturned by the secret ways of Thy adorable Providence!

Before I left Grenoble, that good girl I have spoken of came to me weeping, and told me I was going and hid it from her, because I would have nobody know it· but that the devil would be before me in all the places I should go to; that I was going to a town where·I would scarce be arrived before he would stir up the whole town against me, and would do me all the harm he possibly could. What obliged me to conceal my departure was fear of being loaded with testimonies of friendship from a number of good persons, who had a great affection for me.

I embarked then upon the Rhone, with my maid and a young woman of Grenoble the Lord had favored through my means. The Bishop of Grenoble's Almoner also accompanied me, with another worthy ecclesiastic. We met with many alarming accidents and wonderful preservations; but those instant dangers which affrighted others only augmented my peace. The Bishop of Grenoble's Almoner was much astonished. He was in a desperate fright, when the boat struck against a rock, and opened; and in his emotion looking attentively at me, he observed that I did not change my countenance, or move my eye-brows, retaining all my tranquility.

As I was going from Grenoble, a man of quality, a servant of God, and one of my intimate friends, had given me a letter for a knight of Malta, who was devout, and whom I had esteemed as a man whom our Lord designed to serve the order of Malta greatly, and to be its ornament and support by his holy life. I had told him that I thought he should go thither, and that God would assuredly make use of him to diffuse a spirit of piety into many of the knights. So he went to Malta, where the first places were soon given him. This man sent him the little book of prayer written by me. He had a chaplain averse to the spiritual path. He took this little book, and condemning it, went to stir up a part of the town, and among the rest the seventy-two disciples of St. Cyran. I arrived at Marseilles at ten o'clock, and that afternoon all was in a noise against me. Some went to the Bishop, telling him that, on account of that little book, it was necessary to banish me. They gave him the book. He liked it well. He sent for Monsieur Malaval and Father Recollect, to enquire from whence that great tumult had its rise, which made me smile, seeing so soon accomplished what that young woman had foretold. Monsieur Malaval and that good father told the Bishop what they thought; after which he testified much uneasiness at the insult given me, desired me to stay at Marseilles, and assured me he would protect me. He asked where I lodged, that he might come and see me.

At Marseilles, I was instrumental in supporting some good souls, and among others an ecclesiastic, who till then was unacquainted with me. After having finished his thanksgiving in the church, seeing me go out, he followed me into the house in which I lodged, telling me the Lord inspired him to address me, and open his inward state to me. The Lord gave him through me all that was necessary for him, from whence he was filled with joy and thankful acknowledgment to God.

From Marseilles I knew not whither I should turn. I saw no likelihood either of staying or of returning to Grenoble, where I left my daughter in a convent. Father La Combe had written he did not think I ought to go to Paris. One morning I felt inwardly pressed to go somewhere. I took a litter to go to the Marchioness of Prunai, the most honorable refuge for me in my present condition. I thought I might pass through Nice on my way to her habitation. But when I arrived at Nice, the litter could not pass the mountain to go thither. I knew not what to do, being here alone, forsaken of everybody, and not knowing what God required of me. My confusion and crosses seemed daily to increase. I saw myself, without refuge or retreat, wandering as a vagabond.

Nothing seemed harder than this wandering life to me, who naturally loved propriety and decorum. In this uncertainty, not knowing what course to take, one came to tell me that next day a sloop would set off, to go in one day to Genoa; and they would land me at Savona, from whence I might get myself carried to the Marchioness of Prunai's house. To that I consented. There came a tempest in a dangerous place, and the mariners were of the wickedest. The irritation of the waves gave a satisfaction to my mind. I pleased myself in thinking that those mutinous billows might supply me with a grave. Those with me took notice of my intrepidity, but knew not the cause. I asked of Thee, my Love, some little hole of a rock to be placed in, there to live separate from all creatures. But Thou designed me a prison far different from that of the rock, and quite another banishment than that of the uninhabited island. Calumnies proved the unrelenting waves to which I was to be exposed, to be lashed and tossed by them without mercy. By the tempest swelling we were kept back, and instead of a day's passage to Genoa, we were eleven days in making it. We could not land at Savona. We were obliged to go on to Genoa. We arrived there the week before Easter.

I was obliged to bear the insults of the inhabitants, caused by the resentment they had against the French, for the havoc of a late bombardment. The Doge was newly gone out of the city, and had carried with him all the litters. I could not get one, and was obliged to stay several days at excessive expenses, for the people demanded as much for every single person as they would have asked for a company at the best eating-house in Paris. I had little money left, but my store in Providence could not be exhausted. By the force of entreaty they brought me a sorry litter with lame mules, and told me that they would take me to Verceil, two days' journey, but demanded an enormous sum; they would not take me to the Marchioness of Prunai's house, as they knew not where her estate lay. This was a strong mortification, for I was unwilling to go to Verceil; nevertheless the proximity of Easter and want of money, in a country where they used every kind of extortion and tyranny, left me no choice but to be thus conveyed to Verceil.

Thus Providence led me whither I would not. Our muleteer was one of the most brutal men, and seeing he had only women under his care, he used us in the most insolent and boorish manner.

We passed through a wood infested with robbers. The muleteer was afraid, and told us that if we met any of them on the road we should be murdered, for they spared nobody. Scarcely had he uttered these words when there appeared four men well armed. They stopped the litter. The man was exceedingly frightened. I made a light bow of my head, with a smile, for I had no fear. I had no sooner saluted them, than God made them change their design. Having pushed off one another, as it were, to hinder each of them from doing any harm, they respectfully saluted me, and with an air of compassion retired. I was struck to the heart, O my Love, with a clear conviction that it was a stroke of Thy right hand, who had other designs over me than to suffer me to die by the hand of robbers.

The muleteer, instead of taking me to the inn, brought me to a mill, in which there was not one woman, and but one chamber with several beds in it, in which the millers and muleteers lay together. In that chamber they forced me to stay. I told the muleteer I was not a person to lie in such a place, and wanted him to take me to the inn; but nothing of it would he do. I was constrained to go out on foot, at ten at night, carrying a part of my clothes, more than a quarter of a league in the dark, in a strange place, not knowing the way, crossing one end of the wood infested with robbers, to get to the inn. That fellow hooted after us in an abusive manner. I bore my humiliation cheerfully, but not without feeling it. We were well received at the inn; and the good people did the best in their power for our recovery from fatigue. They assured us the place we had left was dangerous. Next morning we were obliged to return on foot to the litter, for that man would not bring it to us. He fell on us with a shower of fresh insults. To consummate his base behavior he sold me to the post, whereby I was forced to go the rest of the way in a post-chaise instead of a litter.

In this equippage I arrived at Alexandria, a frontier town, subject to Spain, on the side of the Milanese. Our driver took us to the post-house. I was exceedingly astonished when the landlady came out to oppose his entrance. She had heard there were women in the chaise, and taking us for a different sort of women protested against our coming in. The driver was determined to force his entrance. Their dispute rose to such a height that a great number of the officers of the garrison, with a vast mob, gathered at the noise, who were surprised at the woman refusing to lodge us. I entreated the post to take us to some other house, but he would not. He assured the landlady we were persons of honor and piety. By force of pressing entreaties, he obliged her to come to see us. As soon as she looked at us, she acted as the robbers had done; she relented at once and admitted us.

No sooner had I alighted than she said: "Go shut yourselves in that chamber, and do not stir, that my son may not know you are here; for as soon as he knows it he will kill you." The two poor girls who were with me were under frightful apprehensions. When any came to open the door, they thought they were coming to kill them. They continued in a dreadful suspense, between life and death, till next day, when we learned that the young man had sworn to kill any woman who lodged at the house; because a few days before an event had fallen out which had liked to have ruined him: a woman of bad life having there privately murdered a man, that cost the house a heavy fine; and he was afraid of any more such persons coming, and not without reason.

CHAPTER XXVI.

After such adventures, and others tedious to recite, I arrived at Verceil. I went to the inn, where I was badly received. Father La Combe came in a strange fret at my arrival. He could not hide it from me. He said that everyone would think I was come after him, and that would injure his reputation, which in that country was high. I had no less pain to go thither. Necessity only obliged me to submit to such a disagreeable task. I told him if he required me to return, I would go off that moment, however oppressed and spent, both with fatigues and fastings. He replied he did not know how the Bishop of Verceil would take my arrival, after he had given over all his expectations of it, and after I had so long and obstinately refused the obliging offers he had made me, since which he no longer expressed any desire to see me.

It seemed as if I were rejected from the face of the earth, without being able to find any refuge, and as if all creatures combined to crush me. I passed that night without sleep, not knowing what course I should be obliged to take, being persecuted by my enemies and a disgrace to my friends.

When it was known at the inn that I was one of Father La Combe's acquaintance, they treated me with the greatest kindness, for they esteemed him as a saint. As soon as the Bishop knew I was arrived, he sent his niece, who took me in her coach to her house; but only out of ceremony, and the Bishop knew not what to think of a journey so unexpected, after I had thrice refused, though he sent expresses on purpose to bring me. He was out of humor with me. Nevertheless, as he was informed that my design was not to stay at Verceil, but to go to the Marchioness of Prunai's house, he gave orders for me to be well treated. He could not see me till Easter Sunday was over. Then he came to me at his niece's home, and though he understood French as little as I did Italian, he was well satisfied with the conversation, and appeared to have as much favor for me as he had indifference before. The second visit gained him entirely.

He conceived a strong friendship for me, as if I had been his sister; and his only pleasure, amid his continual occupations, was to pass half an hour with me in speaking of God. He wrote to the Bishop of Marseilles to thank him for having protected me in the persecutions there. He wrote to the Bishop of Grenoble; he omitted nothing to manifest his affection for me. He seemed to think alone of finding out means to detain me in his diocese. He would not hear of my going to see the Marchioness of Prunai. He wrote to her to come and settle with me in his diocese. He sent Father La Combe to her to exhort her to come, assuring her he would unite us all to make a congregation. The Marchioness entered into it, and so did her daughter. They would have come with Father La Combe, but the Marchioness was sick. The Bishop was active in establishing a society, and found several pious persons and some devout young ladies, who were ready to join us. But it was not the will of God to fix me thus, but to crucify me yet more.

The fatigue of traveling made me sick. The girl whom I brought from Grenoble fell sick. Her relations took it in their heads that, if she should die in my service, I would get her to make a will in my favor

Her brother, full of this apprehension, came with all speed; and the first thing he spoke to her about, though he found her recovered, was to make a will. That made a great noise in Verceil; for he wanted her to return with him, but she refused. I advised her to do what her brother desired. He contracted a friendship with some of the officers of the garrison, to whom he told ridiculous stories. They gave out that I was come after Father La Combe. They persecuted him on my account. The Bishop was troubled, but could not remedy it. The friendship he had for me increased every day; because, as he loved God, so he did all those whom he thought desired to love Him.

Father La Combe was his prebend and his confessor. He esteemed him highly. God made use of him to convert several of the officers and soldiers, who became patterns of piety. Everything was mixed with crosses, but souls were gained to God. Some of his friars advanced toward perfection. Though I neither understood their language nor they mine, the Lord made us understand each other in what concerned His service. The Rector of the Jesuits took his time, when Father La Combe was gone out of town, to prove me. He had studied theology, which I did not understand. He propounded several questions. The Lord inspired me to answer him so that he went away surprised and satisfied.

Father de la Mothe tried to draw Father La Combe to preach at Paris. He wrote to the Father-General, saying they had no one at Paris to support their house, that it was a pity to leave such a man as Father La Combe in a place where he only corrupted his language; that it was necessary to make his fine talents appear at Paris, where he himself could not bear the burden of the house, if they did not give him an assistant of such qualifications. Who would not have thought all this to be sincere? The Bishop of Verceil, a friend to the Father-General, having advice thereof, opposed it.

The Father-General of the Barnabites would not agree to the request of Father de la Mothe, for fear of offending the Bishop of Verceil. My indisposition increased. The air caused me a continual cough, with fever. I grew so much worse it was thought I could not get over it. The Bishop was much afflicted to see it, but, having consulted the physicians, they assured him that the air of the place was mortal, whereupon he said with many tears: "I would rather have you live, though distant from me, than see you die here. In the diocese of Geneva, they persecuted and rejected you; and I, who would gladly have you, can not keep you." He wrote to Father de la Mothe that I should go in the spring, as soon as the weather would permit; he was exceedingly sorry to let me go; he had looked upon me as an angel in his diocese, and other things enough to have thrown me into confusion, if could have attributed anything to myself. He still hoped to have kept Father La Combe, which probably might have been had not the death of the Father-General given it another turn.

Here I wrote on the Apocalypse, and the great certainty of all the persecution of the most faithful servants of God.

The Bishop of Verceil's friend, the Father-General of the Barnabites, departed this life. As soon as he was dead, Father de la Mothe wrote to the Vicar-General, renewing his request to have Father La Combe as an assistant, and hearing that I was obliged on account of indisposition to return to France, he sent an order to Father La Combe to return to Paris, and accompany me in my journey thither, as his doing that would exempt their house at Paris, already poor, from the expenses of so long a journey. Father La Combe, who did not penetrate the poison under this fair outside, consented thereto, and went off twelve days before me, to transact some business, and wait for me at the passage over the mountains, where I had most need of an escort. I set off in Lent, the weather being fine. It was a sorrowful parting to the Bishop. I pitied him; he was so much affected at losing both Father La Combe and me. He caused me to be attended, at his own expense, as far as Turin, giving me a gentleman and one of his ecclesiastics to accompany me.

As soon as the resolution was taken that Father La Combe should accompany me, Father de la Mothe reported that he had been obliged to do it, to make him return to France. He expiated on the attachment I had for Father La Combe, pretending to pity me for it. They said that I ought to put myself under the direction of Father de la Mothe. He deceitfully palliated the malignity of his heart, writing letters full of esteem to Father La Combe, and some to me of tenderness, desiring him to bring his dear sister, and serve her in her infirmities, and in the hardships of so long a journey; that he should be sensibly obliged to him for his care; with many other things of like nature.

I could not resolve to depart without going to see the Marchioness of Prunai, notwithstanding the difficulty of the roads. She was extremely joyful at seeing me. She acknowledged that all I had told her had come to pass. We made ointments and plasters together, and I gave her the secret of my remedies. I encouraged her, and so did Father La Combe, to establish an hospital in that place; which was done while we were there. My enemies made use of that afterwards.

As soon as it was determined that I should come into France, the Lord made known to me it was to have greater crosses than ever. Father La Combe had the like sense. He encouraged me to resign myself to the Divine will, and to become a victim offered freely to new sacrifices. He wrote: "Will it not be a thing glorious to God, if He should make us serve in that great city, for a spectacle to angels and to men?" I set off then with a spirit of sacrifice, to offer myself up to new kinds of punishments, if pleasing to my Lord. I could not forbear to testify it to my most intimate friends, who tried hard to prevail on me not to proceed further. They were all willing to contribute to my settlement there, and prevent my coming to Paris. But I found it my duty to hold on my way, and to sacrifice myself for Him who first sacrificed Himself for me.

At Chamberry we saw Father de la Mothe. Though he affected an appearance of friendship, it was not difficult to discover that his thoughts were different from his words, and that he had conceived dark designs against us. I speak not of his intention, but to obey the command given me to omit nothing.

Scarcely had I arrived at Paris, when I discovered the black designs entertained against Father La Combe and me. Father de la Mothe, who conducted the whole tragedy, artfully dissembled; flattering me to my face, while aiming the keenest wounds behind my back. He and his confederates wanted to persuade me to go to Montargis (my native place), hoping to get the guardianship of my children, and dispose of my person and effects. All the persecutions from Father de la Mothe and my family and those against Father La Combe have sprung from rage and revenge, because he, as my director, did not oblige me to do what they wanted, as well as out of jealousy.

I arrived in Paris on Magdalene's eve, 1686, exactly five years after my departure. After Father La Combe arrived, he was soon followed and much applauded. I perceived some jealousy in Father de la Mothe hereupon, but did not think that matters would be carried so far. The greater part of the Barnabites of Paris joined against Father La Combe. But all their calumnies were overthrown by the unaffected piety he manifested, and the good multitudes reaped from his labors.

Father de la Mothe and the Provincial, acting as persons well affected to the church, knew I had been at Marseilles, and thought they had a good foundation for a fresh calumny. They counterfeited a letter from a person at Marseilles, addressed to the Archbishop of Paris, in which they wrote the most abominable scandal. Father de la Mothe came to draw me into his snare, and to make me say in the presence of the people he had brought, that I had been at Marseilles with Father La Combe. "There are," said he, "shocking accounts against you, sent by the Bishop of Marseilles. You have there fallen into great scandal with Father La Combe. There are good witnesses of it." I replied with a smile: "The calumny is well devised, but it would have been proper to know first whether Father La Combe had been at Marseilles, for I do not believe he was ever there in his life. While I was there, Father La Combe was laboring at Verceil." He was confounded and went off, saying: "There are witnesses of its being true." He went to ask Father La Combe if he had not been at Marseilles. He answered him he had never been there. They were struck with disappointment. They then gave out that it was not Marseilles but Seisel.

Seisel is a place where I have never been, and there is no Bishop there.

Every device was used to terrify me by threats, forged letters, and memorials drawn up against me, accusing me of teaching erroneous doctrines, of living a bad life and urging me to flee the country to escape the consequences of exposure; but failing in all these, at length Father de la Mothe took off the mask, and said to me in the church before Father La Combe: "You must flee; you are charged with crimes of a deep dye." I was not moved in the least, but replied with my usual tranquility: "If I am guilty of such crimes I can not be too severely punished; wherefore I will not flee. But if I am innocent, for me to flee is not the way for my innocence to be believed."

Similar attempts were made to ruin Father La Combe. He was grossly misrepresented to the king, and an order procured for his imprisonment in the Bastile.

Although on his trial he appeared quite innocent, yet they made the king believe he was a dangerous man in the article of religion. He was shut up in a fortress of the Bastile for life; but as his enemies heard that the captain in that fortress esteemed him and treated him kindly, they had him removed to a much worse place. God will reward every man according to his works. I know by an interior communication he is well content, and fully resigned to God.

Father de la Mothe now endeavored more than ever to induce me to flee, assuring me if I went to Montargis, I should be out of all trouble; but if I did not, I should pay for it. He insisted on my taking himself for my director, to which I could not agree. He decried me wherever he went, and wrote his brethren to do the same. They sent me abusive letters, assuring me that if I did not put myself under his direction I was undone. I have the letters still. One father desired me in this case to make a virtue of necessity. Nay, some advised me to pretend to put myself under his direction and to deceive him, whereas I abhorred the thought of deceit. At church I heard people behind me exclaim against me, and some priests say it was necessary to cast me out of the church. I left myself to God without reserve, being ready to endure the most rigorous tortures, if such were His will.

I never made any solicitation either for Father La Combe or myself, though charged with that among other things. Willing to owe everything to God, I have no dependence on any creature. I would not have it said that any but God had made Abraham rich (Gen. xiv. 23). To lose all for Him is my best gain; and to gain all without Him would be my worst loss. Although so general an outcry was raised against me, God used me to gain many souls to Himself. The more persecution raged against me the more children were given me, on whom the Lord conferred great favors.

One must not judge of the servants of God by what their enemies say of them, nor by their being oppressed under calumnies. Jesus Christ expired under pangs. It will only be seen in eternity who are the true friends of God. Nothing pleases Him but Jesus Christ, and that which bears His character.

They were continually pressing me to flee, though the Archbishop had bidden me not to leave Paris. But they wanted to give the appearance of criminality both to me and to Father La Combe by my flight. They knew not how to make me fall into the hands of the official. If they accused me of crimes, it must be before other judges; and any other judge would have seen my innocence, and the false witnesses would run the risk of suffering for it. They continually spread stories of horrible crimes; but the official assured me that he had heard no mention of any, for he was afraid I would retire out of his jurisdiction. They made the king believe I was an heretic; that I carried on a literary correspondence with Molinos (I never knew there was one in the world, till the Gazette told me); that I had written a dangerous book, and it would be necessary to issue an order to put me in a convent; that, as I was a dangerous person, it would be proper for me to be locked up, since I continually held assemblies, which was false. To support this calumny my handwriting was counterfeited, and a letter was forged importing that I had great designs, but feared they would prove abortive, through the imprisonment of Father La Combe, for which reason I left off holding assemblies at my house, being too closely watched; but that I would hold them at the houses of other persons. This forged letter they showed the king, and an order was given for my imprisonment.

This order would have been put in execution two months sooner had I not fallen sick. Some thought I had a gathering in my head. The pain I suffered for five weeks made me delirious. I had also a pain in my breast and a violent cough. Twice I received the holy sacrament, as I was thought to be expiring. One of my friends acquainted Father de la Mothe (not knowing him to have had any hand in Father La Combe's imprisonment) that she had sent me a certificate from the inquisition in Father La Combe's favor, having heard that his was lost. They had made the king believe that he had run away from the inquisition; but this showed the contrary.

Father de la Mothe then came to me, when I was in

excessive pain, counterfeiting all the affection in his power, and telling me the affair of Father La Combe was going on well; that he was ready to come out of prison with honor; that he was glad of it; that if he had only this certificate, he would soon be delivered. I ordered it to be given him. But he suppressed it, and gave out that it was lost. It never could be got from him. The Ambassador from the Court of Turin sent a messenger to me for this certificate, designing to serve Father La Combe. I referred him to Father de la Mothe. The messenger went to him and asked for it. He denied I had given it to him, saying: "Her brain is disordered, which makes her imagine it." The man came back and told me. The persons in my chamber bore witness that I had given it to him. Yet all signified nothing; it could not be got out of his hands; he insulted me, and caused others to do it, though I was so weak that I seemed at the gates of death.

They told me they only waited for my recovery to cast me into prison. He made his brethren believe that I treated him ill. They wrote me that I was mad and ought to be bound, and a monster of pride, since I would not suffer myself to be conducted by Father de la Mothe. Such was my daily feast in the extremity of my pain; deserted of friends, and oppressed by enemies; the former being ashamed of me, through the calumnies forged and industriously spread; the latter let loose to persecute me; under all of which I kept silence, leaving myself to the Lord.

There was not any infamy, error, sorcery, or sacrilege of which they did not accuse me. As soon as I was able to be carried to the church in a chair I was told to speak to the prebend. (It was a snare concerted between Father de la Mothe and the Canon at whose house I lodged.) I spoke to him with much simplicity, and he approved of what I said. Yet, two days after they gave out that I had uttered many things, and accused many persons; from hence they procured the banishment of sundry persons with whom they were displeased, men of honor of whom I had never heard. One of them was banished because he said my little book was a good one. It is remarkable that, far from condemning the book, it has been reprinted since I have been in prison, and advertisements of it have been posted up at the Archbishop's palace, and all over Paris. In regard to others, when they find faults in their books, they condemn the books and leave the person at liberty; but as for me, my book is approved, sold and spread, while I am kept a prisoner for it.

The day those gentlemen were banished, I received a sealed order to repair to the Convent of the Visitation of St. Mary's, in a suburb of St. Antoine. I received it with a tranquility, which surprised the bearer exceedingly. He could not forbear expressing it, having seen the extreme sorrow of those who were only banished. He was so touched as to shed tears. Although his order was to carry me off directly, he was not afraid to trust me, but left me all the day, desiring me to repair to St. Mary's in the evening. My friends came to see me, and found me cheerful, which surprised them. I could not stand, I was so weak, having the fever every night, it being only a fortnight since I was thought to be expiring. I imagined they would leave me my daughter and maid to serve me. My daughter was most at my heart. I had endeavored to root out her faults, and dispose her to have no will of her own; the best disposition for a child. She was not yet twelve.

CHAPTER XXVII.

January 29th, 1688, I went to St. Mary's. They let me know I must neither have my daughter nor a maid, but be locked up alone in a chamber. It touched me to my heart when my daughter was taken from me. They would neither allow her to be in that house, nor anybody to bring me any news of her. The people of the house were prepossessed with so frightful an account of me that they looked at me with horror. For my jailor they singled out a nun who would treat me with the greatest rigor.

They asked me who was now my confessor. I named him, but he was seized with such a fright that he denied it, though I could have produced many persons who had seen me at his confessional. They said they had caught me in a lie. My acquaintance said they knew me not, and others were at liberty to say all manner of evil of me. The woman, my keeper, was gained over by my enemies, to torment me as an heretic, an enthusiast, one crack-brained and an hypocrite. God alone knows what she made me suffer.

Monsieur Charon, the official, and a doctor of Sorbonne came four times to examine me. Our Lord did me the favor He promised to His apostles: to make me answer much better than if I had studied (Luke xxi. 14, 15). They said if I had explained myself in the book entitled, "Short and Easy Method of Prayer," as I now did, I would not now have been here. My last examination was about a counterfeit letter. I told them the hand was no way like mine. They said it was only a copy; they had the original at home. I desired a sight of it, but could not obtain it. I told them I never wrote it, nor did I know the person to whom it was addressed, but they took no notice of what I said.

After this letter was read, the official said: "You see, madam, after such a letter there was foundation enough for imprisoning you." "Yes, sir," said I, "if I had written it." I showed them its falsehoods and inconsistencies, but in vain. I was left two months, and treated worse and worse, before either of them came again to see me. Till then I had always some hope that, seeing my innocence, they would do me justice; but I saw they did not want to find me innocent, but to make me appear guilty.

The official alone came the next time, and told me I must speak no more of the false letter; that it was nothing. "Nothing," said I, "to counterfeit a person's writing, and make one appear an enemy to the State!" He replied: "We will seek out the author of it." "The author," said I, "is no other than the Scrivener Gautier." He then demanded where the papers were I wrote on the Scriptures. I told him I would give them up when I should be out of prison, but was not willing to tell with whom I had lodged them.

I had an inexpressible joy in suffering as a prisoner. The confinement of my body made me better relish the freedom of my mind. St. Joseph's day was a memorable day, for my state had more of heaven than of earth. This was followed with a suspension of every favor then enjoyed, a dispensation of new sufferings. I was obliged to sacrifice myself anew, and to drink the very dregs of the bitter draught.

I never had any resentment against my persecutors, though I well knew them, their spirit and their actions.

Jesus Christ and the saints saw their persecutors, and saw that they could have no power except it were given them from above (John xix. 11).

Loving the strokes God gives, one can not hate the hand which He makes use of to strike with

A few days after, the official came, and told me he gave me liberty to go and come in the house. They were now industrious in urging my daughter to consent to a marriage which, had it taken place, would have been her ruin. They placed her with a relation of the gentleman whom they wanted her to marry. All my confidence was in God, that He would not permit it to be accomplished, as the man had no tincture of Christianity, being abandoned both in principles and morals.

To induce me to give up my daughter they promised me an immediate release from prison and from every charge under which I labored. But if I refused, they threatened me with imprisonment for life, and death on the scaffold. In spite of all their promises and threatenings, I persistently refused.

Soon after, the official and doctor came to tell the prioress I must be closely locked up. She told them the chamber I was in was small, having an opening to the light or air only on one side, through which the sun shone all the day, and being July, it must soon cause my death. They paid no regard thereto. She asked why I must be thus closely locked. They said I had committed horrible things in her house, even within the last month, and had scandalized the nuns. She protested the contrary, and assured them the whole community had received great edification from me, and could not but admire my patience and moderation. It was all in vain. The poor woman could not refrain from tears at a statement so remote from the truth.

They then sent for me, and told me I had done base things in the last month. I asked: "What things?" They would not tell me. I said that I would suffer as long and as much as it should please God; that this affair was begun on forgeries, and so continued; that God was witness of everything. The doctor told me that to take God for a witness in such a thing was a crime. I replied: "Nothing in the world can hinder me from having recourse to God." I was then shut up more closely than at first, until I was absolutely at the point of death, being thrown into a violent fever, and almost stifled with the closeness of the place, and not permitted to have any assistance.

In the time of the ancient law, the Lord's martyrs suffered for asserting and trusting in the one true God. In the primitive Church of Christ the martyrs shed their blood, for maintaining the truth of Jesus Christ crucified. Now there are martyrs of the Holy Spirit, who suffer for their dependence on Him, for maintaining His reign in souls, and for being victims of the Divine will.

It is this Spirit which is to be poured out on all flesh. The martyrs of Jesus Christ have been glorious martyrs, he having drank up the confusion of that martyrdom; but the martyrs of the Holy Spirit are martyrs of reproach and ignominy. The devil no more exercises his power against their faith or belief, but directly attacks the dominion of the Holy Spirit, opposing His celestial motion in souls. Oh, Holy Spirit of love, let me ever be subjected to Thy will, and, as a leaf is moved before the wind, so let me be moved by Thy Divine breath. As the impetuous wind breaks all that resists it, so break Thou all that opposes Thy empire.

Although I have been obliged to describe the procedure of those who persecute me, I have not done it out of resentment, since I love them and pray for them, leaving to God the care of defending me and delivering me out of their hands, without any movement of my own.

August 22nd, 1688, it was thought I was about coming out of prison. But the Lord gave me a sense that, far from being willing to deliver me, they were only laying new snares to ruin me, and make Father de la Mothe known to the king and esteemed. On this day, my birthday, being forty years of age, I awaked under an impression of Jesus Christ in agony, seeing the counsel of the Jews against Him. I knew that none but God could deliver me out of prison, and I was satisfied that He would do it one day by His own right hand, though ignorant of the manner, and leaving it wholly to Himself.

My case was laid before Madame de Maintenon, who became deeply interested and at length procured my release, and a few days afterward I had my first interview with Abbe Fenelon.

Coming out of St. Mary's I retired into the community of Madame Miramion. In this house my daughter was married to Monsieur L. Nicholas Fouquet, Count de Vaux. I removed to my daughter's house, and on account of her youth lived with her two years and a half, but even there my enemies were ever forging one thing after another against me. I wanted to retire secretly to the house of the Benedictines at Montargis, but it was discovered, and both friends and enemies jointly prevented it.

The family in which my daughter was married being of the number of Abbe Fenelon's friends, I often saw him at our house. We had some conversations on the subject of a spiritual life, in which he made objections to my experiences. I answered with my usual simplicity, which gained upon him. As the affair of Molinos made a great noise, the plainest things were distrusted, and the terms used by mystic writers exploded. But I so clearly expounded everything to him, and so fully solved all his objections, that no one more fully imbibed my sentiments than he, which laid the foundation of that persecution he suffered. His answers to the Bishop of Meaux show this.

I took a little private house, to follow the inclination I had for retirement, where I sometimes had the pleasure of seeing my family and a few friends. Certain young ladies of St. Cyr having informed Mad. Maintenon, that they found my conversation attracted them to God, she encouraged me to continue my instructions to them; and by the change in some of them with whom before she had not been well pleased, she found she had no reason to repent of it. She then treated me with much respect, and for three years after I received from her every mark of esteem and confidence. But that afterward drew on me the most severe persecution. The free entrance I had into the house, and the confidence which some young ladies of the Court, distinguished for their rank and piety, placed in me, gave no small uneasiness to the people who had persecuted me. The directors took umbrage at it, and under pretext of the troubles I had had some years before, they engaged the Bishop of Chartres, Superior of St. Cyr, to present to Madame Maintenon that I troubled the order of the house, and that the young women in it were so attached to me that they no longer hearkened to their superiors. I went no more to St. Cyr.

I fell sick. The physicians, after trying in vain the usual method of cure, ordered me to repair to the waters of Bourbon. My servant had been induced to give me poison. I suffered such exquisite pains that, without speedy succor, I should have died. The man ran away, and I have never seen him since. When at Bourbon, the waters I threw up burned like spirits of wine. The waters had little effect. I suffered from it above seven years.

God kept me in such a disposition of sacrifice that I was quite resigned to receive from His hand all that might befall me, since to offer in any way to vindicate myself would be only beating the air. When the Lord is willing to make anyone suffer, He permits even the most virtuous people to be readily blinded toward them; and the persecution of the wicked is but little compared with that of the servants of the Church, deceived and animated with a zeal they think right.

At this time I had my first acquaintance with the Bishop of Meaux. I gave him the history of my life, and he confessed that he found therein such an unction as he had rarely done in other books, and that he had spent three days in reading it, with an impression of God on his mind all that time.

I proposed to the Bishop to examine all my writings, which he took four or five months to do, and then advanced all his objections, to which I gave answers; but from his unacquaintance with the interior paths, I could not clear up all the difficulties he found in them.

I pray God with my whole heart sooner to crush me utterly, with the most dreadful destruction, than to suffer me to take the least honor to myself of anything which He has been pleased to do by me for the good of others. I am only a poor nothing. God is all-powerful. He delights to operate and exercise His power by mere nothings.

The first history of myself was short. In it I particularized my faults and sins, and said little of the favors of God. I was ordered to burn it, write another, and in it omit nothing anyway remarkable that had befallen me. I did it. It is a crime to publish the secrets of the king, but it is good to declare the favors of the Lord and magnify His mercies.

As the outcry against me became more violent, and Madame Maintenon was moved to declare against me, I sent to her through the Duke of Beauvilliers, requesting the appointment of proper persons to examine my life and doctrines, offering to retire into any prison until fully exculpated. My proposal was rejected. In the meantime one of my most intimate friends, Monsieur Fouquet, was called away by death. I felt his loss deeply. He was a true servant of God.

Being now determined to retire out of the way of giving offense to any, I wrote to some of my friends and bade them a last farewell, not knowing whether I were to be carried off by the indisposition which I then labored under, which had been a constant fever for forty days past, or to recover.

Referring to the Countess of G. and the Duchess of M., I wrote: "When these ladies and others were in the vanities of the world, when they patched and painted, and some of them were in the way to ruin their families by gaming and profusion of expense in dress, nobody arose to say anything against it; they were quietly suffered to do it. But when they have broken off from all this, then they cry out against me as if I had ruined them. Had I drawn them from piety into luxury, they would not make such a cry. The Duchess of M. at her giving herself up to God, thought herself obliged to quit the Court, which was to her like a dangerous rock, in order to bestow her time on the education of her children and the care of her family, which she had neglected. I beseech you, therefore, to gather all the memorials you can against me, and if I am found guilty of the things they accuse me of, I ought to be punished."

I sent them my two little printed books, with my commentaries on the Holy Scriptures. I also wrote a work to facilitate their examination, and spare them as much time and trouble as I could, which was to collect a great number of passages out of approved writers, which showed the conformity of my writings with those used by the holy penmen. I caused them to be transcribed by the quire, as I had written them to send them to the three commissioners. This work was entitled, "The Justifications." It was composed in fifty days, and appeared sufficient to clear up the matter. But the Bishop of Meaux would never suffer it to be read.

After all the examinations, and making nothing out against me, who would not have thought but they would have left me in peace? But the more my innocence appeared, the more did they, who had undertaken to render me criminal, put every spring in motion to effect it. I offered the Bishop of Meaux to go to any community in his diocese, that he might be better acquainted with me. He proposed St. Mary de Meaux, which I accepted; but going thither in the depth of winter I had like to have perished in the snow, being stopped four hours in a deep hollow. I was drawn out at the coach door with my maid. We sat upon the snow, and expected nothing but death. I never had more tranquility of mind, though chilled and soaked with snow. Occasions like these show whether we are perfectly resigned to God. This poor girl and I were in a state of entire resignation, though sure of dying if we passed the night there, and seeing no likelihood of anyone coming to our succor. At length some waggoners came up, who with difficulty drew us through the snow.

The Bishop was astonished, and had no little self-complacency to think I had thus risked my life to obey him so punctually, yet afterward denounced it as artifice and hypocrisy.

There were times when I found nature overcharged; but the love of God and His grace rendered sweet to me the worst of bitters. His invisible Hand supported me, else I had sunk under so many probations. Sometimes I said: "All thy waves and thy billows are gone over me" (Psa. xlii. 7). "He hath bent his bow and set me as a mark for the arrow. He hath caused the arrows of his quiver to enter into my reins" (Lam. iii. 12, 13). It seemed as if everyone thought he was in the right to treat me ill, and rendered service to God in doing it. I then comprehended that it was the manner in which Christ suffered. He was numbered with the transgressors (Mark xv. 28). He was condemned by the sovereign pontiff, chief priests, doctors of the law, and judges deputed by the Romans, who valued themselves on doing justice. Happy they who by suffering for the will of God have so near a relation to the sufferings of Jesus Christ!

For six weeks after my arrival at Meaux, I was in a continual fever, nor had I recovered, when I was waited on by the Bishop, who would fain have compelled me to give it under my hand that I did not believe the Word incarnate (or Christ manifest in the flesh). I answered him that through the grace of God, I knew how to suffer, even to death, but not how to sign such a falsehood.

The Bishop brought me a confession of faith to sign, promising to give me a certificate which he had prepared; but on my delivering him my submission signed, he refused the certificate. Some time after, he endeavored to make me sign his pastoral letter, and acknowledge that I had fallen into those errors he there lays to my charge, threatening me with those persecutions I afterwards endured, in case of non-compliance. I continued refusing to put my name to falsehoods. After I had remained about six months at Meaux he gave me the certificate, but finding Madame Maintenon disapproved of the certificate he had granted, he wanted to give me another in place of it. My refusal to deliver up the first certificate enraged him, and as I understood they intended to push matters with the utmost violence, I took the resolution of continuing in Paris in some private place with my maids, who were trusty; to hide myself from the world. I continued thus five months. I passed the day all alone in reading, in praying to God, and in working. But December 27th, 1695, I was arrested, though exceedingly indisposed at that time, and conducted to Vincennes. I was three days in the custody of Monsieur des Grez, who had arrested me, because the king would not consent to my being put into prison, saying several times over, that a convent was sufficient. They deceived him by still stronger calumnies. They painted me in colors so black that they made him scruple his goodness and equity. He then consented to my being taken to Vincennes.

I shall not speak of that long persecution, which has made so much noise, for a series of ten years, imprisonments in all sorts of prisons, and of a banishment almost as long, and not yet ended, through crosses, calumnies, and all imaginable sorts of sufferings. There are facts too odious which charity induces me to cover.

I have borne long and sore languishings, and oppressive and painful maladies without relief. I have been also inwardly under great desolations for several months, in such sort that I could only say these words: "My God, my God, why hast Thou forsaken me!" All creatures seemed to be against me. I then put myself on the side of God against myself.

Perhaps some will be surprised at my refusing to give the details of the greatest and strongest crosses of my life, after I have related those which were less. I thought it proper to tell something of the crosses of my youth, to show the crucifying conduct which God held over me. I thought myself also obliged to relate certain facts, to manifest their falsehood, the conduct of those by whom they had passed, and the authors of those persecutions of which I have been only the accidental object, as I was only persecuted, in order to involve therein persons of great merit; whom, being out of their reach by themselves, they, therefore, could not personally attack, but by confounding their affairs with mine. I thought I owed this to religion, piety, my friends, my family, and myself.

While I was a prisoner at Vincennes, I passed my time in great peace. I sang songs of joy, which the maid who served me learned by heart, as fast as I made them; and we together sang thy praises, O my God! The stones of my prison looked like rubies; I esteemed them more than all the gaudy brilliancies of a vain world. My heart was full of that joy which Thou givest to them who love Thee, in the midst of their greatest crosses.

When things were carried to the greatest extremities, being then in the Bastile, I said to Thee: "O my God, if Thou art pleased to render me a new spectacle to men and angels, Thy holy will be done!"

DECEMBER, 1709.

Here her story ends. She lived a retired life above seven years. What she had written being only done in obedience to the commands of her director. She died June 9th, 1717, at Blois, being seventy years old.

THE END.

A PRISONER'S SONG.

[While a prisoner at Vincennes, in 1698, Madame Guyon wrote this beautiful hymn.]

A little bird I am,
  Shut from the fields of air;
And in my cage I sit and sing
    To Him who placed me there;
Well-pleased a prisoner to be,
Because, my God, it pleases Thee.

Nought have I else to do;
  I sing the whole day long;
And He whom well I love to please
    Doth listen to my song;
He caught and bound my wandering wing,
But still He bends to hear me sing.

Thou hast an ear to hear,
  A heart to love and bless;
And though my notes were e'er so rude,
    Thou wouldst not hear the less;
Because Thou knowest, as they fall,
That love, sweet love, inspires them all.

My cage confines me round,
  Abroad I can not fly;
But though my wing is closely bound,
    My heart's at liberty;
My prison walls can not control
The flight, the freedom of the soul.

Oh! it is good to soar
  These bolts and bars above,
To Him whose purpose I adore,
    Whose Providence I love;
And in Thy mighty will to find,
The joy, the freedom of the mind.